EXTRAS FROM

EXODUS

BIBLE STUDY AIDS *of William G. Heslop*

EXTRAS FROM
EXODUS

by
William G. Heslop, D.D., Litt.S.D.

KREGEL PUBLICATIONS
Grand Rapids, Michigan 49501

Library of Congress Catalog Card Number: 75-13662
ISBN 0-8254-2826-2

First Edition. 1931
Kregel Publications Edition 1975

Printed in the United States of America

CONTENTS

PART II — POINTS FOR EMPHASIS

HOW TO STUDY THE BIBLE

"SEARCH THE SCRIPTURES"

S-e-a-r-c-h

> This word literally means
> "Ransack the Scriptures"
> "Explore the Bible."

S-e-a-r-c-h

1. Systematically

> "Study to shew thyself approved unto God, a workman that needeth not to be ashamed, rightly dividing the word of truth" (2 Tim. 2: 15).

2. Earnestly

> "Open thou mine eyes, that I may behold wondrous things out of thy law" (Psa. 119: 18).

3. Affectionately

> "Make me to understand the way of thy precepts: so shall I talk of thy wondrous works" (Psa. 119: 27).

4. Regularly

> "Blessed is the man that walketh not in the counsel of the ungodly, nor standeth in the way of sinners, nor sitteth in the seat of the scornful: but his delight is in the law of the Lord; and in his law doth he meditate day and night. And he shall be like a tree planted by the rivers of water, that bringeth forth his fruit in his season; his leaf also shall not wither; and whatsoever he doeth shall prosper" (Psa. 1: 1-3).

5. Carefully and Conscientiously

"All scripture is given by inspiration of God, and is profitable for doctrine, for reproof, for correction, for instruction in righteousness: That the man of God may be perfect, throughly furnished unto all good works" (2 Tim. 3: 16, 17).

6. Humbly

"Humble yourselves therefore under the mighty hand of God, that he may exalt you in due time" (1 Peter 5: 6).

Avoid the grasshopper method of Bible study. Read the Bible as you read a love letter.

OTHER METHODS OF BIBLE STUDY

1. The Synthetic Method.

Begin at Genesis and read it through several times. This is study by Books.

2. The Parallel Method.

Study by references. Use the "Treasury of Scripture Knowledge" a book which treats every word in the Bible by references.

The best commentary on the Bible is the Bible itself.

3. The Topical Method.

Bible study by Topics. The "New Topical Text Book" will help you.

4. The Microscopic Method.

This method is accomplished by using a good concordance such as "Clarke's Bible Concordance", "Cruden's", "Young's" or "Strong's."

5. **The Expository Method.**

This is by far the best method of Bible Study. Read

the first chapter of Matthew, making your own notes. Examine the writings of others on the chapter.

There are other profitable methods of Bible study, but the Synthetic - Expository Method is without doubt the best. Avoid the Grasshopper-Capsule-Sermonizing Method of Bible study.

a cluster of jewels
to enrich your Christian
pilgrimage

THE KEY WORD OF EXODUS IS REDEMPTION

1. Redemption through Blood.
        Coverings of skins.
        Abel's lamb.
        Isaac's ram.
        Abraham's heifer.
        Passover lamb.
2. Redemption through Power.
        Plagues.
        Death of first born.
        Red Sea divided.
        Pharaoh destroyed.
3. Redemption through Faith.
        Adam *accepted* the coverings of skins.
        Abel *took* a lamb.
        Israel *sprinkled* the blood.
4. Redemption through the Holy Spirit.
        He moved upon the chaos of Gen. 1: 2.
        Came upon Gideon and Samson.
        Filled Bezaleel.
        The Pillar of cloud and fire which guided Israel.
5. Redemption through obedience.
        Noah *built* the Ark.
        Abraham *offered* Isaac.
        Israel *Obeyed*.
        FAITH WITHOUT WORKS IS DEAD
6. Redemption through discipline.
        Abraham in Egypt.
        Isaac digging Wells.
        Jacob at Bethel.
        Jacob and Laban.
        Jacob at Peniel.
        Moses 40 years in the desert.
        Israel at Shur (No Water).
        Israel at Marah (Bitter Water).

"The book of Exodus is a great turning point in the history of the Old Testament. The family becomes a nation and the nation is set apart for a peculiar, divine purpose. Biographies and family records end, the patriarchal dispensation closes and God is revealed as the God who loves the whole world."

"Here is the Bible. As made up of paper and leather, it is temporal and will perish. Its pages will turn yellow and its cover will wear out. But THERE IS WITHIN THIS BOOK A HIDDEN MEANING that compares to the spirit in man: there is here the unseen Word of God that will never perish."

J. B. CHAPMAN, D. D.

PART I

INTRODUCTORY NOTES

1

CHIEF TOPICS IN EXODUS

I. The Oppression (Bondage).
 1. The enmity of Pharaoh.
 2. The wiles of Pharaoh (Compromises).
 3. The persistence of Pharaoh.
II. The Judgments (Plagues).
 1. Water into blood.
 2. Frogs.
 3. Lice.
 4. Flies.
 5. Murrain.
 6. Boils.
 7. Hail.
 8. Locusts.
 9. Darkness.
 10. Death of the first born.
III. The Passover (Blood).
 1. A lamb.
 2. Without blemish.
 3. A Male.
 4. Young.
 5. Kept until 14th day.
 6. Slain.
 7. Blood shed.
 8. Blood sprinkled.

9. Roast with fire.
10. Israel feasted on the lamb.
    (1) Staff in hand.
    (2) Loins Girt.
    (3) Shoes on feet.
11. Not a bone of the lamb broken.
12. Not sodden at all with water.
    Christ was denied a drop of water when on the cross. There is not a drop of water in hell.

IV. The Law (Obedience).
    1. Thou shalt have no other gods before me.
    2. Thou shalt not make unto thee any graven image, or any likeness of any thing that is in the heaven above, or that is in the earth beneath, or that is in the water under the earth: Thou shalt not bow down thyself to them, nor serve them: for I the Lord thy God am a jealous God, visiting the iniquity of the fathers upon the children unto the third and fourth generation of them that hate me: and shewing mercy unto thousands of them that love me, and keep my commandments.
    3. Thou shalt not take the name of the Lord thy God in vain; for the Lord will not hold him guiltless that taketh his name in vain.
    4. Remember the sabbath day, to keep it holy. Six days shalt thou labour, and do all thy work: But the seventh day is the sabbath of the Lord thy God; in it thou shalt not do any work, thou, nor thy son, nor thy daughter, thy manservant, nor thy maidservant, nor thy cattle, nor thy stranger that is within thy

gates: for in six days the Lord made heaven and earth, and sea, and all that in them is, and rested the seventh day: wherefore the Lord blessed the sabbath day, and hallowed it.

5. Honour thy father and thy mother: that thy days may be long upon the land which the Lord thy God giveth thee.

6. Thou shalt not kill.

7. Thou shalt not commit adultery.

8. Thou shalt not steal.

9. Thou shalt not bear false witness against thy neighbour.

10. Thou shalt not covet thy neighbour's house, thou shalt not covet thy neighbour's wife, nor his manservant, nor his maidservant, nor his ox, nor his ass, nor anything that is thy neighbour's.

This law was

    (1) Given at Sinai.
    (2) Spoken by God.
    (3) Given to Moses.
    (4) Written by the finger of God.
    (5) Is a schoolmaster.
    (6) Reveals the holiness of God.
    (7) Demands a perfect righteousness.
    (8) Shows the exceeding sinfulness of Sin.
    (9) Reveals man's helplessness.
    (10) Proves the need of *INWARD* holiness.

V. The Tabernacle (Worship).

    1. The Court.

        (1) Gate.
        (2) Brazen Altar.
        (3) Laver.

2. The Holy Place.
    (1) The Candlestick.
    (2) The Table of Bread.
    (3) The Vail.
3. The Holy of Holies.
    (1) The Golden Altar.
    (2) The Ark.
    (3) The Mercy Seat.

"The Bible is not a worn-out Book yet. The Statue of Liberty in the Harbour of New York, lifts its great light for the guidance of mariners, and, though the birds of the night fling themselves madly against its crystal, as if to put out its flame, they only beat themselves into insensibility, and fall dead at its base; so. whatever antagonism there may be to this, God's Beacon Light, those who assault it will only damage themselves, while the light shines on, safe and serene!"

"This Bible is a book which has been refuted, demolished, overthrown, and exploded more times than any other book you ever heard of. Every little while somebody starts up and upsets this book; and it is like upsetting a solid cube of granite. It is just as big one way as the other; and when you have upset it, it is right side up, and when you overturn it again, it is right side up still."

DR. H. L. HASTINGS.

2

MOSES

Exodus is the book of Redemption.

The word Exodus means "Going Out," i. e., exit, departure.

The book records the departure of the children of Israel from Egypt.

There are two outstanding men (1) Moses; (2) Aaron, both of whom act in the place of God.

All the books of the Bible are linked together by words such as THEN or NOW or AND, thus showing that the Bible is one grand and glorious whole. Exodus is linked to Genesis by the word *NOW*. Leviticus is linked to Exodus by the word *AND*. Deuteronomy is linked to Numbers by the word *THESE*. Joshua is linked to Deuteronomy by the word *NOW*. We should not fail to notice these connecting links.

The book of Exodus begins by giving the names of the children of Israel, who came out of Egypt. In process of time Joseph died and there arose a new king over Egypt who knew not Joseph. (All human help must fail and the best of men are forgotten.) When God called Abraham out of Ur of the Chaldees HE promised that his seed should be as the DUST of the EARTH for multitude and as numerous as the SANDS upon the seashore. On another occasion Abraham was promised that his seed should be as the STARS OF HEAVEN. Two seeds were thus promised to Abraham:

(1) A dust seed or earthly people.

(2) A star seed or heavenly people.

The DUST seed refers to Israel as God's earthly people.

17

The STAR seed refers to the Church as God's heavenly people. As time rolled on the children of Israel became more and mightier than the Egyptians; therefore the Egyptians set over them task-masters to afflict them with burdens. The more they afflicted them, however, the more they multiplied and grew. The King of Egypt ordered the Hebrew midwives to kill every baby boy that should be born. The midwives refused to obey the wicked orders of the king, but saved the men children alive. When Pharaoh discovered that his diabolical plans had been frustrated, he charged all his people to cast every son that was born into the river.

This introduces us to the thrilling story of the birth, life, and labors of Moses, who became, under God, one of earth's noblest men. Moses was saved from death when a child. He lived in a palace and gave it up to suffer with the people of God. From his palace he saw his own brethren bowed down with burdens. Moses became one with them in order to deliver them. He was first rejected by his own; was a prophet, a priest, and a ruler; was drawn out of death; out of a palace to a life of loneliness and suffering; drawn out to be a leader, and, finally, drawn out from the world and taken up to heaven fifteen hundred years before his time. (For the first four thousand years of the history of the human family all who died went DOWN. Enoch, Elijah, and Moses alone in Old Testament history went UP.) Moses was rejected by his brethren, but, while he was in rejection, he married a Gentile bride. He was the loneliest man in all the Old Testament. He was slandered, abused, misunderstood, and despised by his own. He was falsely accused and spoken against by his own brethren and on one occasion, at least, they attempted to stone him to death. Notwithstanding all their wickedness, Moses loved them, suffered for them, interceded for them, saved them from Pharaoh and Egypt, and became their law-giver. He died on top of a mountain, and, three days later, was resurrected, and was taken to Paradise above. He has been back to earth since his death and resurrection, and, in all probability, will be one of the two witnesses who will appear on the earth before the final winding up of the affairs of men. Moses was thus a marvelous picture of our Lord Jesus Christ. The points of resemblance are:

1. He lived in a palace.
2. He gave it up to suffer.
3. He gave it up to suffer with the people of God.
4. He was saved from death when a child.
5. He saw his own people bowed down with heavy burdens.
6. He became one with them to save them.
7. He was rejected.
8. He was a lonely sufferer.
9. He was slandered and misunderstood.
10. He was stoned.
11. He was a prophet, a priest, and a king.
12. He died upon a mountain.
13. He was resurrected.
14. He returned to earth again after his resurrection.

The second coming of Moses was certainly a beautiful foreshadowing of the second coming of Christ.

3

BONES AND HOOFS

God heard the groaning of the children of Israel, remembered His covenant with Abraham, Isaac, and Jacob, looked upon them and had respect unto them. Moses kept the flock of Jethro, his father-in-law. The angel of the Lord appeared unto Moses in a flame of fire out of the midst of a bush, and the bush burned with fire, but was not consumed. God had come down to deliver the children of Israel and bring them unto a land flowing with milk and honey. This angel of the Lord who appeared to Moses was none other than our Lord Jesus Christ. (See "Gems from Genesis" by the present writer.)

God thus appeared to Moses, called him to deliver Israel and to lead them out of Egypt into their promised land. At his own request Moses was given a helper in the person of Aaron his brother. Moses and Aaron stepped into the palatial home of Pharaoh, and, in the name of the Lord, requested Pharaoh to allow the children of Israel to hold a feast unto the Lord in the wilderness. Pharaoh refused to allow Israel to leave Egypt, and hardened his heart against God. Here is the beginning of the hardening process which landed Pharaoh into the sea of perdition.

1. Pharaoh refused to make any inquiry into the claims of Moses or Israel or God.
2. He was a cruel and murderous despot.
3. He hardened his own heart against God and against the claims of God.
4. He refused his weary subjects leisure for either worship or rest.

5. He demanded an impossible obedience.
6. He insulted God and insulted God's prophet.
7. He resisted evidence as well as the experience and the testimony of his own priests.
8. He sinned against God.
9. He sinned against Moses.
10. He sinned against humanity.
11. He hardened his own heart in the first place.
12. God hardened his heart and he perished in his sin.

His unclean lips were closed in death and the once proud, boasting, blaspheming Pharaoh was wrapped in a watery shroud and is now a helpless, impotent, mummified corpse.

It does not pay to go against God.

Pharaoh, having refused to listen either to God or Moses, is visited by divine judgment. One plague is followed by another until the wicked king discovers that he is in the hands of a greater than Moses. Pharaoh then seeks to compromise with Moses (1) by having the Children of Israel worship God in the land of Egypt. When this compromise was refused it was then suggested (2) that they do not go very far away. Pharaoh wants to keep them within easy reach of his presence and power. When this compromise is rejected Pharaoh suggests (3) that the men go and worship, but that the children be left behind in Egypt. When this compromise was flatly refused Pharaoh agreed (4) that the men could go with their wives and children, but that they must leave their possessions in Egypt. Moses replied that they not only must all go out of Egypt to worship the Lord, but that all their cattle also must go with them—*"there shall not an hoof be left behind."*

When Joseph was dying in Egypt, he took an oath of the children of Israel saying, "God will surely visit you and ye shall carry up my bones from hence." Joseph died, was embalmed, and was put in a coffin in Egypt. When Israel left

Egypt they digged up the bones of Joseph, carried them across the red sea, through the wilderness to Kadesh, and, after forty years of wandering in the wilderness, Israel crossed the Jordan, and Joseph's bones were buried in Canaan. Not a hoof of Israel and not a bone of Joseph was left behind in Egypt.

Egypt is a type of this present evil world, a place of darkness, bondage, and slavery, receiving no gentle showers from the skies, feeding on onions, leeks, and garlic which grow in the dirt, and can only be obtained by stooping and digging in the ground. Compare this with the food of Canaan such as grapes, figs, and pomegranates which grow in the heavens (atmosphere), and can only be obtained by straightening up and stretching out and pulling. If we would obtain and enjoy the fruits of Canaan, we must straighten up and stretch out and pull. Egypt is thus a picture of this present evil world which keeps the people of God in bondage.

Pharaoh is a type of the devil. He was willful, wicked, rebellious, murderous, and blasphemous; he was a liar and a cruel despot, refusing to give his subjects permission to leave him; he was a hard task master, scheming and planning the destruction of the people of God; he was determined to keep them in his own hands, and in his own power. When he finds he cannot keep them, attempting to deceive them by compromises, he is destroyed by the power of God and sinks into a sea of perdition. The king of Egypt is thus a remarkable type of Satan, the enemy of God and the deceiver of men. If Satan cannot drive us into sin he will attempt to make us compromise. He will seek to persuade us:

1. To stay in the world and still worship the Lord.
2. Not to go far away.
3. To leave our children in the world.
4. To leave our possessions.

Satan knows that if we stay in the world it will not be long before we are acting like the world. The reply of Moses to Pharaoh must be our reply to all the attempts and attacks and compromises of Satan, NOT AN HOOF shall be left behind. If we thus decide that not a hoof shall be left behind, then, when Jesus comes again, He will take our bones up and out of this Egyptian world. Every saint will be resurrected and raptured when Jesus comes again and we shall meet him in the air. Not a bone or hoof shall be left behind. Let us all decide that not an hoof shall be left behind NOW, and, if we thus decide, not a bone shall be left behind in the resurrection morning.

———————•———————

"There are lives so great that all men must have some familiarity with them, and yet no man has exhausted their study, and no speakers have brought to the thought of their fellows all the facts they inspire. Moses is one of those names! I say it without hesitation, that aside from Jesus Christ, Moses is THE man of the Sacred Word. Peter was not one half so great; Paul was not his peer; and if we are disposed to dispute the claim, it only proves that while none of us know the New Testament too well, many are inexcusably ignorant of the Old, and hence unacquainted with some names that have inspired the past, and will profoundly influence the future.

Moses is not one of those names! He is THE one of them. Ingersoll bleated about his blunders, and more honest and competent critics have and will add their attacks upon his name and the books that bear it; but when Ingersoll is forgotten and Infidelity comes to its grave, Moses will live in the memory of sainted minds, and the angel choirs in their grandest oratorio shall couple his name with that of 'The Lamb'."

4

THE BEGINNING OF MONTHS

The first step in the salvation of the children of Israel from Egypt was the raising up of a deliverer. The second step was the determination that not a hoof should be left behind. The next step had to do with the slaying of an innocent lamb. Every man was to take a lamb, a male of the first year without blemish, and test it; then kill it in the evening. They were to take of the blood and strike it on the two side posts and on the upper door posts of their houses. The flesh having been roasted with fire, was to be eaten with unleavened bread. They, with their loins girded, with shoes on their feet, and with staff in their hand were to eat the lamb, and they were to eat it in haste for it was the Lord's passover. The blood was upon the houses for a token, and, on seeing the blood, the destroying angel would pass over. In order to apply the blood upon the side and upper door posts they were to take a bunch of hyssop, dip it in the blood, and strike the lintel and two side posts with the blood. They were to remain under the protection of the blood of the lamb all through the night until the morning. This experience was to be the beginning of months for Israel. It was to constitute their birthday as a nation. Their previous history was to be blotted out and forgotten. A new era was to begin. It was to be the beginning of months for the people of God.

All these things were but shadows and were written for our learning. The LAMB was a type of Christ, "the Lamb of God which taketh away the sin of the world." Innocent, harmless, unoffensive, meek and lowly, the LAMB was led to the slaughter and opened not its mouth.

The MALE lamb speaks of strength and energy while the female offering speaks of fruitfulness and affection. Christ was not only the strong Son of God, He was also the affectionate, tender, and fruitful One.

The TESTED lamb, tested before it was offered, was a type of Christ, who was tested and tried. Even His enemies admitted that they could find no bruises, cuts, or wounds in Him.

The SLAIN lamb speaks of Christ slain for us. The blood must be shed, for a dead lamb without the blood shedding would never have saved Israel in the Old Testament, nor is it possible for a dead Christ without the shedding of blood to save us today.

The BLOOD APPLIED speaks to us that by the hyssop of repentance and faith, the blood of Christ must be applied to our hearts. Thus the destroying angel will PASS OVER us. Covered, preserved, and protected by atoning blood, we shall escape the wrath of the destroying angel.

The Lamb ROAST with fire typifies the wrath of God that burned against the sin bearer as He hung upon the cross, for "it pleased the Lord to bruise Him." Christ bore the wrath of offended Deity. He was roasted with the fire of divine vengeance because of your sin and mine. He was the Lamb bearing away the sin of the world, and it is now our high privilege to eat of the lamb, for He is the Bread of Life.

EAT the lamb. *Eat His head* and learn wisdom, for Christ is the wisdom of God. He is made unto us WISDOM as well as righteousness and sanctification. *Eat His legs*, and learn to walk even as He walked. *Eat His inward parts* and thus put on bowels of mercies, compassion, sympathy, affection, and tenderness. Israel was to eat the head and legs of the lamb with the purtenance thereof, for, unless we eat of His flesh and drink of His blood, there is no life abiding in us, for His flesh is meat indeed and His blood is drink indeed. All through the night of this present evil age we must stay covered with the precious blood and eat of Christ our Lamb who was slain before the foundation of the world.

GIRDED LOINS speak of service. We are ready to serve.

SHOES on our feet testify that we are ready to go, ready to stay, and ready our place to fill.

STAFF in our hand signifies that we are ready to climb any hill and press our way past any and every obstacle.

THE UNLEAVENED BREAD speaks of our separation from everything that is evil. Having accepted Christ as our own personal Savior, we are ready to serve, ready to climb, ready to go, and separated from all that is wrong; and, with the past blotted out, a new life is commenced, a new era is begun. Born again of the Spirit of God, it is indeed the beginning of months. Satan pulls the wool over the eyes of the sinner, and persuades him that if he becomes a Christian, life will be at an end. The facts are just the reverse. Life in its highest and best sense never really begins until it begins with God and His Christ. Real life, enduring pleasure, and abiding happiness can be found alone in Jesus Christ. There is nothing real, there is nothing satisfying, and there is nothing worth while outside of Jesus Christ. Either while we are living, or when we are dying, or after we are dead, we shall awaken to the fact that outside of Christ all is vanity and vexation of spirit. The time which is spent in Egypt was all wasted time to Israel. The years they spent in serving Pharaoh were all lost and wasted years. God, however, blotted out their past, gave them a new beginning, and He will do the same for us. Israel was saved by a Lamb, saved by blood, saved by faith. "Behold the lamb of God."

"Christ OUR PASSOVER is sacrificed for us" (1 Cor. 5: 7).

"Know ye not that a little leaven leaveneth the whole lump? Purge out therefore the old leaven, that ye may be a new lump, as ye are unleavened. For even CHRIST OUR PASSOVER is sacrificed for us, therefore let us keep the feast" (1 Cor. 5: 6-8). It is next to impossible to understand the New Testament without in some measure understanding the Old Testament. It is impossible to understand the book of Hebrews without first of all grasping the main facts of the books of Exodus and Leviticus. If we fail to understand Exodus 12 it will be impossible for us to understand 1 Cor. 5: 6-8. An understanding of the books of the Pentateuch is an essential to an understanding of the Epistles.

The Passover in the book of Exodus, according to the apostle Paul, was a shadow of the great substance, our Lord Jesus Christ. Israel was saved by a lamb, the best and the most perfect of its kind. The Lamb was tested and proved, it was slain, and its blood shed in Egypt, which is a type of the world. The blood of the lamb was applied to their houses. Entering in through blood sprinkled doors and covered by the blood of the lamb, they feasted on the lamb which had been slain for them. With shoes on their feet, staff in their hand, girdle around their loins, and separated from every thing wrong or evil in the sight of the Lord, they feasted on the lamb. They feasted all during the night and the destroying angel, when he saw the blood, passed over them. Thus their passover was a fore-shadowing of Christ, our Passover, who was sacrificed for us. No strangers could eat or feast on the passover lamb in the Old Testament. Only such as submitted to God were allowed to eat of the lamb. No uncircumcised person could eat of the lamb and it is just the same today. It is necessary to be born again, to submit to God, to walk in the light, and to remain separated from evil if we would partake of the Lord's body worthily.

———————◆———————

"Of all books in the world, the Bible is one which will not yield up its riches and its sweetness except to the diligent and faithful and earnest student. All great works demand long and patient and persevering study. The lesser mind cannot expect to grasp at once the purpose of the greater. Sir J. Reynolds tells us of the profound disappointment with which he first beheld Raphael's great picture of the Transfiguration at the Vatican. It was only as he came again and again, only as he lingered over it and dwelt upon it till the picture took possession of him, that he at last perceived its grandeur and its harmony."—PEROWNE.

"Wonderfully is the Bible adapted to all the varying circumstances and necessities of the believer's life. There is a fulness in it which meets every want, and yet can never be exhausted; an interest ever fresh, ever new. We can never outgrow its help, or reach a stage of spiritual advancement when it can no longer lead us. It ever goes before, drawing out and educating every spiritual perception, satisfying every spiritual need, and yet ever giving us a sense of infinite fulness."

HUGH MACMILLAN.

5

SHUR, MARAH AND ELIM

Pharaoh was glad to let the children of Israel depart from Egypt that they might serve the Lord. Plague after plague had been sent upon him and upon all the land of Egypt. At mid-night the Lord had smitten all the first born in all the land of Egypt, and there was not a house where there was not one dead. In every house in Egypt there was either a dead lamb or a dead first born. The children of Israel were thrust out of Egypt. God put crepe on every door knob in Egypt in order to save His people. God wrapped crepe around a nation in order to deliver His people. Thus Pharaoh was glad not only to let the children of Israel go, but also to give them whatsoever they needed for their journey. God led His people by the way of the wilderness and by the way of the Red sea. He went before them by day in a pillar of cloud and by night in a pillar of fire. Pharaoh decided to give chase. The children of Israel crossed the Red Sea as by dry land, which, the Egyptians assaying to do, were drowned. Miriam and all the women took their timbrels in their hands and went out and danced for joy. Then the children of Israel went out into the wilderness of Shur, and, after journeying in the wilderness for three days, they became thirsty, but found no water. There was no water at Shur. They next came to a place called Marah, and they could not drink of the waters of Marah for they were bitter. The people murmured against Moses who cried unto the Lord and the Lord shewed him a tree, which, when he had cast into the water, the waters were made sweet. They next came to a place called Elim where were twelve wells and seventy palm trees, and they encamped there by the waters. The Shurs and Marahs and Elims must be met in our journey from Egypt (the world) to the Canaan of perfect love.

(1) SHUR. Salvation and singing and shouting are always followed by trials and tests. The first real test that came to Israel after crossing the Red Sea was at Shur. We must be prepared for the tests while we are journeying towards our Canaan (holiness).

(2) MARAH. The word Marah means BITTER. After we leave Egypt or the world there are many bitter things to meet. There are bitter pills to swallow while we are on our way to the promised land, but if we suffer we shall also reign with Him. Moses was told to throw the branch of a tree into the bitter waters and the bitter waters would be made sweet. When we meet with bitter experiences in the justified life we must bring the branch (Christ) of the tree (Calvary) into all our bitter experiences and all our bitternesses will be turned into sweetnesses. When tested and tried, remember that Christ also endured the contradiction of sinners against Himself, and that He kept on His even way, uncomplainingly until the crown was won.

At Marah the water was bitter.
Here is the test of DISAPPOINTMENT.
We ought to learn to change the D to H and make it HIS APPOINTMENT.
Each believer must meet his Marahs.

He must come face to face with bitter experiences in his Christian walk.

God's people were in the path of obedience when they came to Marah and hence the testing was educatory and not punitive.

Chastisements may come when we are out of the path and not following the pillar of cloud by day and fire by night, but Israel were following the pillar. Our Marah's are not necessarily punitive but are placed across our path for our benefit here and hereafter.

(3) ELIM. At Elim there were seventy palm trees and twelve wells of water. The palm trees protected them from the scorching sun, and the wells provided them with an abundance of life refreshing water, sufficient to satisfy their every need. The palm trees speak of victory and joy, and, if we will but press our way past the Shurs and the Marahs, we shall be brought to our Elims. Unmurmuring and uncomplainingly we must press on until we reach our Elim where we may rest and refresh ourselves and thus enjoy victory through the Spirit. What a pity to stop at Shur! What a calamity to stop at either Shur or Marah!

6

MANNA

Israel was not called to Elim, but to Canaan. Elim was just a stopping station and only one of the steps in their walk of faith towards Canaan's happy land; and so they took their journey from Elim and marched into the desert. There was no food in the wilderness, and, instead of praying and trusting God, the people murmured and complained. They were ready to accept the benefits, enjoy the deliverances, and become favorites of heaven, but they would not endure the cross. There was no water at Shur; there was bitter water at Marah; now there is no food for them to eat. In all the tests of the justified life while on the way to Canaan, we should guard against murmuring either against God or against God's people. In these early chapters of Exodus we may tune in to some of the table talks of *the old man,* for murmuring or complaining is OLD MAN talk. The Lord was gracious and merciful. He rained manna from heaven sufficient to satisfy the need of three million people. The *manna* was sent down from heaven and it was sent down in the night. Silent and unseen it fell from heaven. The manna was white, round, sweet, and like coriander seed. It was already promised before it came down and was to be gathered every day early in the morning before the sun waxed hot. There was an abundance for each and all, but it was not to be hoarded by any. It was very nourishing and satisfying, but for the most part it passed away unheeded and despised. Egypt was behind; Canaan was ahead; the desert was around them; heaven above satisfied their need. On the way to

Canaan the people of God were sustained by food sent down from heaven.

The MANNA was a type of Christ, sent down from heaven. He also came down in the night, for it was not only a literal night while the shepherds watched their flocks, but it was also a time of darkness in the moral and spiritual realm. It was indeed night when Jesus was born. Silent, unseen, and unheralded, he was born in a stable and cradled in a manger. For four thousand years before He was born, *all salvation had come out of the stable.* Abel's lamb, Isaac's ram, Abraham's heifer, and all the goats, scapegoats, bullocks, and pigeons, all alike, were stable creatures. How fitting that the Lamb of God should be born in a stable. "Selah."

All salvation for all time both in the Old Testament and the New Testament has thus come out of the stable. Like the manna, Christ had already been promised; for was He not the fulfillment of the promise, the seed through whom all the nations of the earth would be blessed; was He not the promised Shiloh, the Man of Peace; and, was he not the Emmanuel, God with us.

It is important to notice that the manna did not fall on the dirty ground, but came down on the dew. The dew is a beautiful emblem of the Holy Spirit. Christ was born of the Spirit and thus became the Bread of Life as He was already the Bread of angels and the Bread of God.

The manna was WHITE, and Jesus was holy, harmless, and undefiled.

The manna was ROUND. Jesus was without either rough edges or sharp corners that take on such large proportions in our own experience and which are such a hindrance to us and to others.

The manna was like coriander SEED. Christ had life in Himself. Here is the explanation of the parable of the mustard seed. The MUSTARD seed is hot and pungent and has *life* in itself. Our Faith must be a living faith and we must KEEP HOT if we would remove mountains. The manna was not like pebbles, but like seed. It was something with life in itself. Coriander cures gas on the stomach. We need more Manna and less Gas. Selah.

The manna was SWEET. Christ is sweeter than the honey and the honey-comb. "Oh, taste and see that the Lord is good." Vinegar, sour, clabber religion is the devil's religion.

The manna was to be gathered EARLY in the morning. If we are to obtain daily strength for daily need, we must make it our FIRST business every morning of every day to gather our portion of the bread of life before the cares and business of the day rush upon us and rob us of our daily bread.

The manna was NOT to be hoarded. We must not keep Christ to ourselves. We must preach Him to others. It is not possible to gather a sufficient supply on Sunday to satisfy our needs for a week; neither is it possible to gather sufficient in one campmeeting to last until the next campmeeting. We need a daily supply. "Give us this day our daily bread." There is in Christ an abundant supply for each and all.

7

JEHOVAH-NISSI

The children of Israel journeyed from the wilderness and pitched in REPHIDIM. There was no water for the people to drink and instead of trusting God they chided Moses. They became so angry that they were almost ready to stone him. They were, in fact, mad enough to kill him. The Lord instructed Moses to go on before the people, and take his rod and smite the rock in the presence of the people, and immediately there gushed forth enough water to satisfy the need of all Israel. THEN came Amalek and fought against Israel in Rephidim. Moses ascended the mountain and stood on the top of the hill with the rod of God in his hand. Joshua with his sword and a number of chosen warriors fought against Amalek, while Moses, Aaron and Hur, went to the top of the hill. When Moses held up his hands in intercessory prayer Israel prevailed, and when Moses let down his hands Amalek prevailed. Moses sat down on the top of the mountain and Aaron and Hur held up his hands. Amalek was finally discomfited and overcome. Doom was pronounced upon Amalek. Moses built an altar and called the name of it Jehovah-Nissi, which means "The Lord Is My Banner." Egypt is a type of the world, Pharaoh is a type of the devil, Moses is a type of Christ, Joshua is a type of Christ in the Spirit, and the sword is a type of the Word of God.

Pharaoh tried to kill Israel in Egypt, and now Amalek tries to kill them in the wilderness.

The rock is a type of Christ, and the smitten rock is a type of Christ crucified. The water is a type of salvation through the Holy Spirit and was made possible through the smiting of the rock.

Moses, on the mountain, is a type of Christ, who ascended on high and ever liveth to make intercession for us. Amalek is a type of the flesh and of the devil.

The word Amalek means to *lick up* or *exhaust*. Satan will seek to stop us, lick us up, and cause exhaustion before we reach Canaan. We need our Moses (Christ interceding) and our Joshua (the Holy Spirit) and our sword (the Word of God) and prayer (Aaron and Hur) or the flesh will devour us and the devil kill us before we reach the happy land of Canaan.

The manna (Christ) came down, the rock (Christ) was smitten, the water (the Holy Spirit) was given THEN Amalek (the devil) was stirred and the war began. It is just the same today. While we journey on towards our Canaan of perfect love, the flesh and the devil will be stirred, and we shall only conquer by relying upon Christ's intercession for us, and by using the Sword of the Spirit, which is the Word of God, and THEN Jehovah-nissi shall be our banner. Praise the Lord.

Jehovah Nissi is one of seven compound names found in the Bible. These seven compound names set forth the glorious theme of salvation from start to finish. They reveal God as meeting every need of man from his lost estate through sin to the end of his pilgrim's progress and the coming of the Lord.

Jehovah is one of the distinctive names of deity as in covenant relation with His people. God is not only the creator, preserver, ruler, redeemer, provider and king, but He has condescended to enter into mutual understanding with His redeemed people. He has made a covenant with them and ratified it by an oath.

The first of the compound names found in the Bible is Jehovah-Jireh. Jehovah-Jireh means "the Lord will provide." Abraham was to offer his only son. The father and son journeyed together to the mount of sacrifice. Carrying the wood upon his own shoulder, the submissive and obedient son of the loving father wended his lonely way up the mount of sacrifice. A ram was caught in the thicket and became a substitute for Isaac. The Lord Jehovah thus provided a sacrificial substitute instead of Isaac. Jehovah-Jireh—"The Lord will provide," became a living reality to Abraham. Thus we have two Old Testament pictures of the New Testament Christ: First, the Son, and second, our substitute, the ram in the thicket. The Son was obedient even unto death, and the harmless, innocent ram died that another might live. Jehovah-Jireh—"the Lord will provide." He provided a covering of skins for our first parents. He provided a shelter for Noah and his house. Jehovah-Jireh—"the Lord will provide." He provided a substitute instead of Isaac. He provided for the needs of the thirsty Israelites by giving them water out of the flinty rock. He provided bread from heaven for three million men, women, and children. He provided the brazen serpent for the plague stricken people in the wilderness. Jehovah-Jireh—"the Lord will provide." He has provided salvation so rich, so full, so free, and so perfect that humans such as we should rend the heavens with shouts of victory and glad hallelujahs, and then go forth to every man of Adam's race to make such a salvation known. This salvation is so grand, so glorious, so satisfying, so abundant, and so great that the question ought to be asked in every land, "How shall we escape if we neglect so great salvation?"

The second compound name is Jehovah-Rapha. Jehovah-Rapha means "the Lord that healeth." God's people had left Egypt and crossed the Red Sea. They had come to Shur where there was no water to drink and had already arrived at Marah. Here there was water, but they could not drink of these waters for they were bitter. The Lord showed Moses a tree which, when cast into the waters, they would be made sweet.

It was immediately after this experience at Marah that God said, "I am the Lord that healeth thee" (Exodus 15: 26). Here is the Jehovah-Rapha, "the Lord that healeth." That this refers to physical healing is undoubtedly true, but the deeper healing of the soul is also implied. It is never wise to limit the scriptures. Jehovah-Rapha takes in spirit, soul, and body. While journeying from Egypt, headed for Canaan's happy land, God will smash a hole in our Red Sea, and make a way where there is no way, and, if we will but bring the tree called Calvary and fling it into the bitter water of our trials and tests which we meet in our every day life, God will turn all our bitternesses into sweetnesses. Jehovah-Jireh—"the Lord will provide." Jehovah-Rapha—"the Lord that healeth."

The third compound name is Jehovah-Nissi. Jehovah-Nissi means "the Lord our banner." God's people thirsted for water. Instead of praying and believing, they murmured against their leader and against their Lord. The Lord in wondrous grace told Moses to take his rod and smite the rock. Moses lifted the rod and smote the rock, forthwith there came waters enough to satisfy the need of three million men, women, and children. At this point Amalek came forth against Israel. Moses ascended the mountain and stood with up-lifted hands on the top of the hill. Aaron and Hur held up his holy hands without wrath and doubting. Joshua with his sword and his soldiers fought against Amalek in the valley, and Amalek was signally defeated. Moses built an altar and called the name of it Jehovah-Nissi—"the Lord is our banner." The Rock of Ages was smitten nineteen hundred years ago, and from the side of that smitten rock there flowed a stream that even now can satisfy the needs of a thirsty world. Your thirsty soul may be satisfied. The rock has been smitten. The water of life is yours for the asking. Come and drink. Jehovah-Jireh—"the Lord will provide." Jehovah-Rapha—"the Lord that healeth." Jehovah-Nissi "the Lord is our banner."

Our Moses, who is Christ, is now on High where "He ever liveth to make intercession for us." Our Joshua, the Holy Spirit is even now in the valley with the sword of God's word, and, together with Hurs and Aarons of prayer, victory will surely perch on our banner, for Jehovah-Nissi—"the Lord is our Banner." The fight is on. Our Moses is on high. Our Joshua is now here. By prayer and faith the victory is ours for Jehovah-Nissi is our banner. Jehovah-Jireh—"the Lord will provide"; Jehovah-Rapha—"the Lord our healer"; and Jehovah-Nissi—"the Lord our banner."

The fourth compound name is Jehovah-Shalom which means "the Lord our peace." God's people in the Old Testament compromised and consequently became captives. The enemy robbed them of their bread and fruit, and left them without sustenance. They cried unto the Lord and the Lord raised up Gideon to be their savior. Gideon was a poor boy. His parents knew what poverty meant. He was the least in his father's house. In wondrous grace God gave him a sign by touching the rock and bringing fire out of the rock. Gideon built an altar and called it Jehovah-Shalom—"the Lord our peace." With his three hundred minute men blowing trumpets, smashing pitchers, and giving a mighty shout that was heard in three worlds, Israel was free. Compromise always ends in captivity. The enemy still delights in driving us and depriving us of our bread of life, and still seeks to destroy our fruit, which is love, joy, and peace. In condescending love God still waits to be gracious. He still gives us water, fire, and honey out of the rock. The rock that was smitten will still give its waters of regeneration and refreshing. There is today holy, sanctifying fire ready to start from the Rock of Ages at the touch of believing prayer. Today those who will blow their trumpets of testimony, who will break their pitchers and shout in the face of every foe, victory will surely perch on their banners. Hallelujahs, persistent testimonies, and shouts will today bring victory to the people of God. Jehovah-Jireh—"the Lord will provide"; Jehovah-Rapha—"the Lord our healer"; Jehovah-Nissi—"the Lord our banner"; and Jehovah-Shalom—"the Lord our peace."

The fifth compound name is Jehovah-Ra-ah. Jehovah-Ra-ah means "the Lord my shepherd." Christ is said to be the *good* shepherd, giving His life for the sheep. Christ is also said to be a *great* shepherd perfecting the sheep for whom He died. Christ is not only the good shepherd and the great shepherd, but is also the *chief* shepherd, and in one of God's tomorrows will come again to receive His own. As the good shepherd he died. As the great shepherd he lives. As the chief shepherd he will come again. Jehovah-Ra-ah—"the Lord my Shepherd." Not only *a* shepherd, but *my* shepherd. Not only *the* shepherd, but *my* shepherd. Jehovah-Jireh — "the Lord will provide"; Jehovah-Rapha—"the Lord our healer"; Jehovah-Nissi—"the Lord our banner"; Jehovah-Shalom— "the Lord our peace"; Jehovah-Ra-ah—"the Lord my Shepherd."

This brings us to Jehovah-Tsidkenu. Jehovah-Tsidkenu means "the Lord our righteousness." The Lord provided a sacrificial lamb and became our Jehovah-Jireh. Through the bloody tragedy of Golgotha, healing for spirit, soul, and body was made possible, and thus the Lord became our Jehovah-Rapha. In the battle against sin, Satan, the world, and the flesh, the Lord becomes our Jehovah-Nissi. He is our peace and thus our Jehovah-Shalom. He is my shepherd and thus my Jehovah-Ra-ah. He will yet be our Jehovah-Tsidkenu. Jehovah-Tsidkenu thus points us to a coming king. Christ was a prophet. He now is a priest, and He will be a king. Jehovah-Tsidkenu—"the Lord our righteousness." Jehovah-Tsidkenu thus sets forth the fact that all our righteousness is as filthy rags, that salvation is all of grace. Jehovah-Tsidkenu points onward and forward to the coming king. "Let not your heart be troubled: ye believe in God, believe also in me. In my Father's house are many mansions: if it were not so, I would have told you. I go to prepare a place for you. And if I go and prepare a place for you, I will come again, and receive you unto myself: that where I am, there ye may be also."

"Why stand ye gazing up into heaven?" said the two men in white apparel, "this same Jesus, which is taken up from you into heaven, shall so come in like manner as ye have seen him go into heaven." Paul, the great apostle to the Gentiles, also reminds us that "the Lord himself shall descend from heaven with a shout, with the voice of the archangel, and with the trump of God: and the dead in Christ shall rise first: Then we which are alive and remain shall be caught up together with them in the clouds." The dead saints shall be resurrected, the living saints shall be raptured, and we shall all meet the Lord in the air and "so shall we ever be with the Lord."

Noah and those saved in the ark not only went up together, but also came back to earth again, and lived and reigned over a purified creation. Isaac was offered as a sacrifice to God, was resurrected in a figure and went back home to await his bride. Joseph suffered innocently. Although at first rejected, he was, in God's good time and way, exalted to a throne. David was despised and rejected of men, a man of sorrows and acquainted with grief. He had not where to lay his head, but David finally was crowned king of all Israel. Just so, our Noah has gone up, our Isaac still awaits his bride, our Joseph is even now seated upon a throne of grace and giving supplies to all who need and seek, our David, once despised and rejected and crowned with thorns, will soon be crowned with glory, and in deed and in truth will be our Jehovah-Tsidkenu, "the Lord our righteousness."

Like the wise virgins we wait with lamps trimmed and burning bright. Our Jehovah-Tsidkenu—"the Lord our righteousness" in the past and present, and our hope for the future, will yet descend, and righteousness shall cover the earth as the waters cover the seas.

The last of these seven compound names is Jehovah-Shammah. Jehovah-Shammah means—"the Lord is present." This sets forth the abiding presence of Christ with His redeemed people. God has always wanted to live with men. He linked arms with our first parents in the garden of Eden. He talked with Enoch and made known His righteous and holy will to Noah. He visited with Abraham under the tree. He wrestled with Jacob, conquered him, and changed his name to Israel, a Prince with God. He came down and dwelt with His people in the tabernacle. He filled the temple with His glory. He made known to Manoah and his wife that a son would be born. He at last came down and was born in a stable and cradled in a manger—Emmanuel, "God with us."

Jehovah-Shammah, "the Lord is present." The four evangelists record the great commission of Christ which He gave before He ascended on high, and assured us in His own words of His presence, "Lo, I am with you alway, even unto the end of the world."

Christ our Jehovah-Jireh — "the Lord will provide"; Christ our Jehovah-Rapha—"the Lord our healer"; Christ our Jehovah-Nissi—"the Lord our banner"; Christ our Jehovah-Shalom—"the Lord our peace"; Christ our Jehovah-Ra-ah—"the Lord our Shepherd"; Christ our Jehovah-Shammah—"the ever-present, abiding Lord of Glory"; and Christ our Jehovah-Tsidkenu—"the Lord our righteousness."

> "We search the world, and truth we cull,
> The good, the pure, the beautiful,
> From graven rock and written scroll,
> And all old flower-fields of the soul:
> And, weary seekers of the best,
> We come back, laden from our quest,
> To find that all the sages said
> Was in the Book our mothers read."

8

GOD'S SANCTUARY

God visited Adam in the garden, walked with Enoch and with Noah, feasted with Abraham, wrestled with Jacob, appeared to Moses in the burning bush, filled the temple with his presence and glory, and came down to be born in a stable and cradled in a manger. He had always planned and purposed to live with men. In the ancient tabernacle in the wilderness He came down and dwelt with Israel. To the end that they might make Him a tabernacle or sanctuary, He invited every man who would to bring an offering. The offering was to be of gold, silver, and brass; and of blue, purple, and scarlet, fine twined linen; and of goats' hair, rams' skins dyed red, and badgers' skins; and wood, oil for the light, and spices for the anointing oil, and for sweet incense, onyx stones, and stones to be set in the ephod and in the breast plate. Thus were they to provide and make a SANCTUARY that God may dwell among them.

This is the first announcement of a fixed, abiding presence of God in the midst of men. The offering was to be a voluntary, free will offering. It was to be spontaneous and from the heart.

The GOLD sets forth the Deity of Christ, for He was truly God. Gold is made by God and comes from God. Man cannot make gold.

The WOOD sets forth the humanity of Christ, for He was truly man and also truly God. Trees grow in the earth, receive a measure of nourishment and support from nature and must be cut down in order to obtain wood. Christ was the Living Tree cut down to provide an ark for Noah and a sanctuary for Israel.

The deity and humanity of Christ was seen throughout all His life and ministry. Asleep on a pillow (humanity), He arose and calmed the stormy sea (deity). Weary and sitting upon a well (human), He told the astonished woman her past life (divine). He wept over Lazarus (human), and then raised him from the dead (divine). He was hungry (human), yet he fed the multitudes (divine). He died (human), and He arose from the dead (divine). He was born in time (human), and yet was from eternity (divine). Thus is seen both the gold (deity) and the wood (humanity).

The SILVER sets forth the redemption that is in Christ Jesus. The tabernacle stood upon silver sockets. The half shekel of silver was atonement money. Both Christ and Joseph were sold for silver; thus silver speaks of Christ's atonement.

The BRASS sets forth the righteousness of Christ. God is not only Light and Love, but He is Holy, Just, and Righteous; thus the brazen altar speaks of righteousness and justice satisfied.

The BLUE sets forth the heavenly Christ. Blue, which is the color of the sky speaks of that which is heavenly in contrast with green, which is the color of the earth and speaks of that which is earthly. The green grass, the green leaves of the trees, and the blue sky all have a message for us. In the book of Revelation there is mention made of a green rainbow. The rainbow speaks of mercy, and the green rainbow speaks of mercy towards the earth. Blue sets forth the heavenly Christ. The blue ribbon brigade in the Old Testament has lessons for us today. Touching the blue hem of His garment revealed healing faith in a heavenly Christ.

The PURPLE speaks of the kingly Christ. Purple is the royal color and sets forth Christ as the King.

The SCARLET speaks of the suffering Christ. Scarlet has reference to the sorrows, the sufferings, the shed blood, and the death of Christ.

The FINE LINEN speaks of the holy life of Christ as He walked the earth. Fine twined linen speaks of the finely woven, regular, even, holy, and spotless earthly life of Christ. There is no animal fat contained in fine twined linen, and herein lies the reason why the officiating priest was not allowed to appear before the Lord in woolen garments. There is a fundamental difference between woolen garments and linen garments. Wool is obtained from an animal and is irritating and sweat producing. Linen is a vegetable substance and does not contain any animal fat. Sweat is the result of sin and therefore the priest was not allowed to appear before the Lord in woolen garments. Every housewife knows that it is almost impossible to wash the grease or fat out of wool. Instead of the soap eating up the fat or the grease of the wool, the wool will eat up the soap. The priests were thus forbidden to appear before God with anything upon them that caused sweat or savored of animalism. There is a profound meaning in all these things.

The GOATS' HAIR speaks of Christ as the separated One. In order to obtain goats' hair, the hair must be separated from the goat. The goat must sacrifice its own covering in order to provide a covering for others. The goat speaks of Christ being made a curse for us. On the cross of Calvary Christ became accursed, for He that hangeth on a tree is accursed of God.

The RAMS' SKINS dyed red speak of Christ as our substitute, consecrating Himself to the death of the cross, and dying in order that we might live. The ram died instead of

Isaac and thus became a substitute for Isaac, and Christ died in our stead and thus became our Substitute.

In order to obtain rams' skins, the innocent rams must die. A ram was caught in the thicket, was placed upon the altar in consecration, and was killed instead of Isaac and thus the ram became a substitute for Isaac. The ram thus fore-shadowed Christ as the substitute, dying, the just for the unjust and the innocent for the guilty. The rams' skins dyed red thus set forth the substitutionary sufferings and death of Christ.

The BADGERS' SKINS speak of Christ as the one in whom there was no form or comeliness. Shoes or sandals were made from the common badger's skin, and badgers' skins were the outer covering for the tabernacle. The rough leather-like outer covering of the sanctuary was unattractive and without beauty, and is it not written that "He was without form or comeliness and there was no beauty in Him that we should desire Him"?

OIL for the light. Oil is one of the emblems of the Holy Spirit. Things mingled with oil set forth the birth of the Spirit. Things with oil poured upon them set forth the baptism with the Spirit. Things anointed with oil set forth separation and fitness for service. Christ was born of the Spirit, filled with the Spirit, and anointed by the Spirit; therefore He was the Light of the world.

The SPICES used in making the anointing oil set forth those qualities of Christ such as gentleness, kindness, affection, love, charity, forbearance, longsuffering, and His gracious winsome, forgiving Spirit.

The SWEET INCENSE sets forth the Holy life of Christ ascending to God as a sweet smelling savor.

The STONES such as the onyx, and stones to be set in the ephod all speak of Christ. Man never made a stone, and

God never made a brick. Nimrod may build his tower with bricks, but God never made a brick nor built anything with bricks nor has He ever ordered anyone else to build anything with bricks. Saints are living STONES and not BRICKS. The sanctuary was God's dwelling place among men, and Christ was the Emmanuel, which means *God with us*.

"There is no finer field for the study of the true nature of worship than the symbolism of the Old Testament, once we penetrate its spiritual meaning.

The writer of the Epistle to the Hebrews proceeds on the basis that Old Testament ritualism was the foreshadowing of Christ and His redemption as revealed in the New Testament. These things, he says, 'serve unto the example and shadow of heavenly things, as Moses was admonished of God when he was about to make the tabernacle: for, See, saith he, that thou make all things according to the pattern shewed to thee in the mount' (Hebrews 8: 5). The word *pattern* as here used signifies literally a type, such as is made by the impression of a stamp or seal. The word is sometimes used by classical writers to denote an outline, such as the sketch used by an artist or architect. In either sense of the term, the tabernacle is to be regarded as a typical building and evidently indicates that a distinct impression of the tabernacle and its furniture was conveyed to the mind of Moses by the great Architect who gave him the pattern in the mount, and charged him to carefulness and precision in the execution of the plans.

Whether the tabernacle be viewed as the world revealing the Father in His eternal power and Godhead; or Christ as the Word incarnate; or the Church as indwelt by the Holy Spirit, its prayerful study yields rich fruitage to the reflective mind."   H. ORTON WILEY.

EIGHT REASONS TO STUDY THE TABERNACLE

1. It holds a large place in the Sacred Scriptures.
   There are thirteen chapters in Exodus,
   eighteen chapters in Leviticus,
   thirteen chapters in Numbers,
   two chapters in Deuteronomy,
   four chapters in Hebrews,
   besides scores of separate verses scattered throughout the New Testament dealing with the tabernacle.
   That which is of such concern to God ought to be of importance to us.

2. God honored the type by rending the veil at the crucifixion of His son.
   "The veil of the temple was rent in twain."

3. The tabernacle clearly typifies the Lord Jesus Christ. Hebrews 10: 20.

4. It was designed and inspired by the Holy Spirit.
   "The Holy Ghost thus signifying that the way into the holiest of all was not yet made manifest" (Heb. 9: 8).

5. It is impossible to understand the Epistle to the Hebrews without understanding the tabernacle.
   In the measure that we understand the tabernacle we shall understand and appreciate Paul's letter to the Hebrews.

6. The study of the tabernacle helps us to appreciate the Person and Work of our Lord Jesus Christ and is a sure antidote to the poison of unsound doctrine as to sin, holiness, atonement, and salvation.

7. It will make us fool proof against the attacks of higher criticism and unbelief.
   Infidelity is insanity.

8. Its teaching and application covers almost the whole range of New Testament doctrine and experience.
   "Whatsoever things were written aforetime were written for our learning" (Romans 15: 4).

9

THE TABERNACLE

THE ARK OF THE COVENANT

"All Scripture is given by inspiration of God, and is profitable . . . that the man of God may be perfect throughly furnished unto all good works" (2 Tim. 3: 16, 17).

"Man shall not live by bread alone, but by every word that proceedeth out of the mouth of God" (Matt. 4: 4).

"Whatsoever things were written aforetime were written for our learning" (Rom. 15: 4).

"All these things happened unto them for ensamples and they are written for our admonition upon whom the ends of the world are come" (1 Cor. 10: 11).

"The law having a shadow of good things to come" (Heb. 10: 1).

The Lord instructed Moses to make an ark or chest of wood and overlay it with pure gold within and without, and make upon it a crown of gold round about, and cast four rings of gold for it, and put the rings in the four corners of the ark. He was also commanded to make staves of wood, and overlay them with gold, and the staves were to be put into the rings by the sides of the ark that the ark might be borne with them throughout their journeys. The unbroken tables of the law or the testimony were to be put into the ark.

There are three arks mentioned in the Bible which were all saving arks.

1. Moses' ark.
2. Noah's ark.
3. The ark of the covenant.

The ark of the covenant was thus a chest made of wood and covered with gold and fixed with rings and staves so that the children of Israel could carry it with them in their journeyings.

The WOOD sets forth the humanity of Christ.

The GOLD sets forth the Deity of Christ.

The CROWN speaks of Christ as the King of Kings and Lord of Lords.

The STAVES speak of Christ as the everliving and ever present Savior, who is with us throughout our wilderness journeyings.

The unbroken TABLES of the law speak of Christ as the One who perfectly kept the law, and kept it for us.

THE MERCY SEAT

Moses was commanded to make a mercy seat of pure gold and two Cherubim made of beaten gold. One cherub was to be made on one end and the other on the other end of the mercy seat. The cherubim were to stretch forth their wings on high, covering the mercy seat with their wings and they were to look the one to the other toward the mercy seat. The mercy seat was to be put above upon the ark. God promised that He would meet His people THERE, and commune with them from above the mercy seat, from between the two cherubim which were upon the ark of the testimony.

The mercy seat was a golden lid that fitted the chest called the ark. It was made of gold and so teaches us that all mercy is divine and comes from God.

The cherubim with the mercy seat were beaten out of one solid piece of gold; thus it sets forth the sufferings of God in order to provide a throne of grace and place of mercy where He could meet with us and have fellowship and communion with us.

Paul speaks of "the cherubim of glory shadowing the mercyseat" (Heb. 9: 5).

The mercyseat, as the Word implies, is a place of mercy and thus foreshadows our Lord Jesus Christ. The mercy seat was the LID belonging to the ark of the covenant which covered the law of God which was in the ark. Here is the reason why some people, lifting the LID from the ark and looking inside, were smitten by God. The law, uncovered by the mercy seat, rose up and smote the intruders. Without the mercy seat (Christ) we are always in danger of being smitten. It was at the mercy seat where perfect atonement was made for all Israel.

THE TABLE OF SHEWBREAD

Moses was commanded by the Lord to make a table of wood, to overlay it with pure gold, to make a crown of gold around about it, to make for it four rings of gold and put them in the four corners, and to make staves in order to carry the table throughout all their wilderness journeyings.

The staves were to be made of wood and overlaid with gold upon which the table of shewbread was to be borne. Dishes, spoons, bowls, and covers were also to be made of pure gold. Shewbread was to be set upon the table before the Lord always.

The WOOD sets forth the humanity of Christ, and the gold sets forth His Deity as the Crown sets forth His Kingship.

The TABLE speaks of fellowship, communion, and feasting.

The SHEWBREAD speaks of Christ as the Bread of God, the Bread of angels, and the Bread of Life to men. He is always with us and satisfies our every need.

THE CANDLESTICK

The Lord commanded Moses to make a candlestick of pure gold. It was to be made of beaten work, the shaft, branches, bowls, knops, and flowers were to be of beaten work of pure gold. Six branches were to come out of the side of the candlestick, three branches out of the one side and three branches out of the other side. The three bowls were to be made like unto almonds with their knops and flowers.

The candlestick was the only light in the holy place. Tongs and snuff dishes also were to be made of pure gold. Everything was to be made according to the pattern which was shown to Moses in the mount.

The CANDLESTICK sets forth Christ as the Light of the World.

The PURE GOLD sets forth His Divinity, and shews that the light is a Divine Light.

The BEATEN work sets forth the sorrows and sufferings of Divinity in order to provide a Light to lighten the Gentiles, and to be the Glory of Israel.

The BRANCHES set forth the church of Christ, which is also the light of the world. Jesus said, "I am the Light of the World," and speaking to His disciples, He said, *"Ye are the light of the world."*

Almonds, knops, and flowers set forth the resurrection, life, and fruitfulness of Christ. It is a well known fact that, in the spring, the almond tree is the first to bud, the first to blossom, and the first to bear fruit.

The TONGS and SNUFF DISHES were to remove the charred wick and soot from the branches of the candlestick.

This sets forth the necessity of the church of Christ being trimmed and cleansed so that the light may burn more brightly.

Thus the candlestick sets forth Christ and His Church. The candlestick was not for show but for light.

The oil in the candlestick sets forth the necessity of being filled with the Spirit as Christ was filled with the Spirit.

The candlestick was to shine in a dark place. The number seven shows that its light was to be a perfect, full, and clear light.

The candlestick was to burn from the evening until the morning. We are to be burning and shining lights until the morning of Christ's coming for His own. The candlestick was the only source of light, and Christ, with His church, is the only Light of the World.

THE BRAZEN ALTAR

Moses was instructed to make an altar of wood, and to make four horns upon the corners thereof and overlay it with brass. He was also to make pans to receive the ashes. All the vessels thereof were to be made of brass. A grate of net work of brass was also to be made with four brazen rings in the four corners thereof. Staves of wood, overlaid with brass, were to be put into the rings in order that the altar might be carried with them in all their journeyings.

There were seven articles of furniture in the tabernacle.
1. The altar of burnt offering or the brazen altar.
2. The laver or wash basin.
3. The table of shewbread.
4. The candlestick.
5. The altar of incense.
6. The Ark of the Covenant.
7. The Mercy Seat.

The brazen altar was the first piece of furniture which a man could see in his approach to the tabernacle.

The *WOOD* sets forth the humanity of Christ and the

Brass sets forth the righteousness of Christ. Justice was satisfied at the Brazen Altar.

Gold, silver, wood, and brass have profound meanings in the Word of God. The *wood* sets forth the human nature of our Lord Jesus Christ who was born in a stable; after the manner of men He was circumcised; he became obedient to his parents; he was tempted and became hungry; we find Him eating with publicans and sinners, paying tribute, weeping over Lazarus and Jerusalem, washing the disciples' feet, and praying all night. We find Him again sleeping on a pillow and weary at a well, falling down while carrying His cross, and dropping agonizing sweat. In all this He was the Word MADE FLESH. *Brass* speaks to us of the righteousness, justice, judgment, and equity of God. Brass is the most unbending and unyielding of all minerals. When Jesus said, "Woe unto thee Chorazin, woe unto thee Bethsaida, woe unto thee Capernaum," He was manifesting the brazen altar part of His work. When He was reproving the Pharisees and ordering the buyers and sellers from the temple and speaking words terrible enough to make one's hair stand up (as, for instance, when he was speaking on the subject of hell) He was showing forth the brass qualities in His nature. The brazen altar thus sets forth the righteousness, justice, and holiness of God satisfied by the death of Christ. This is the first altar, this is the first piece of furniture met with by man in his approach to God.

The *horns* overlaid with brass were for the purpose of binding the victim to the altar. The altar sets forth the cross of Christ. As the victim was bound to the brazen altar, Christ was bound to the cross. The *ashes,* which were received in a pan, set forth the BODY of Christ after He had been burned up as a sacrifice for the sin of the world. Just as the innocent victims in the Old Testament were taken and laid in a clean place, so the ashes of Christ were taken and laid in a clean place, in the new tomb wherein never man was laid. The wood of the brazen altar must have been charred and almost burned to a cinder by the continual fire which burned the victims upon the altar. As our Lord Jesus was hanging upon the cross of Calvary, He too, was a charred mass of bruises and blood. At the brazen altar justice was satisfied; at the cross of Christ the justice and righteousness of God was vindicated and satisfied. The blood of God was shed that we might be redeemed.

THE COURT OF THE TABERNACLE

From fine twined linen Moses was commanded to make hangings for the court of the tabernacle. He was also to make a gate or entrance or door to the court of the tabernacle, and an hanging of blue, purple, and scarlet, fine twined linen wrought with needle work. The hanging was to be supported by four pillars which were to rest in four sockets of brass. All the vessels of the tabernacle and all the pins of the court were to be made of brass.

The FINE TWINED LINEN speaks of the holy, spotless, clean, devoted life of Christ as He walked among men.

The GATE speaks of Christ as the One entrance, the one way into the presence of God. "I am the Way."

The blue of the hanging or gate sets forth the heavenly Christ; the scarlet sets forth the sufferings of Christ; and the fine twined linen, *wrought* with *needle work,* sets forth the *daily life* of Christ. Needle work requires patience and skill; this shows us that the way to God, righteousness, salvation, holiness, and heaven has been made for us through the holy life of our Lord Jesus Christ as well as by His sacrificial death on the cross. We are saved by His life as well as through His death.

There was only one way into the presence of God in Old Testament times and there is only one way into the presence of God in New Testament times. "NO MAN cometh unto the Father but by ME."

THE ALTAR OF INCENSE

The Lord commanded Moses to make an altar of wood overlaid with pure gold upon which he was to burn incense. It was to be four square with horns and golden rings and staves to bear it or carry it with them throughout their journeyings. The staves were to be made of wood overlaid with gold. The altar of incense was to be put before the vail which is by the ark of the testimony and before the mercy seat. THERE the Lord was to meet with *His* people. Aaron was to burn incense upon it every morning and every night. Aaron was also to make an atonement upon the horns of it once in a year with the blood of atonement and it was a thing most holy unto the Lord.

The *wood* of the Altar of Incense sets forth the humanity of Christ and the pure *gold* sets forth His Deity. The blood of atonement sets forth the blood of Christ which was shed on the cross. This altar of Incense was placed before the vail which is by the ark of the testimony, and before the mercy seat which is over the testimony (coming out). There has been almost a universal mistake made in the placing of this altar of incense. Bible students and teachers place this altar of incense in the holy place, whereas it ought to be placed in the holy of holies. The mistake has been made by failing to notice that the *book of Exodus is dealing with God coming out and down to men.*

In the tabernacle God comes out to men, and, in coming out to men, He first of all provided an ark and a mercy seat which typified Jesus Christ. Before God could come out to men there must be an ark and there must be a mercy seat. Not only so, but there must be an altar of incense which typifies the holy, spotless, pure, and perfect life of Christ. This was put *before the vail* that is by the ark of the testimony COMING OUT. The altar of incense was before the mercy seat that is over the testimony COMING OUT. Thus in order to come out to men God must have before Him the ark (Christ) and the mercy seat (Christ) and the altar of incense (the holy life of Christ). All this was necessary before God could come out to men. If we will remember that Exodus is dealing with God COMING OUT to men, the position of this altar will be plain, i. e., before the vail (COMING OUT), before the mercy seat (COMING OUT). The apostle Paul settles this question for all time. Writing to the Hebrews he says, "There was a tabernacle made; the first, wherein was the candlestick, and the table, and the shewbread; . . . and after the second vail, the tabernacle which is called the holiest of all which had the golden censer." Notice carefully the expression:

"THE HOLIEST OF ALL WHICH HAD THE GOLDEN CENSER" (Heb. 9: 2-5).

The seven articles of furniture as arranged in the tabernacle were as follows:

The outer court:
  (1) The brazen altar.
  (2) The laver.

The Holy place:
  (1) The candlestick.
  (2) The table of shewbread.

The holiest of all:
  (1) The ark of the covenant.
  (2) The mercy seat.
  (3) The altar of incense.

Man begins at the brazen altar but God begins with the ark of the covenant.

God began with the perfect, holy Christ in heaven. Man begins with a crucified and cursed Christ on earth.

THE LAVER

Moses was commanded to make a laver of brass with a foot or stand also of brass, and to put water therein in order that Aaron and his sons might wash themselves before they entered into the presence of God.

Absolute purity in the priest was required in order that he might enter into the presence of God on behalf of Israel. Neglect to wash meant death.

In order to obtain an audience with God, absolute purity and perfection was necessary. All this sets forth the purity and perfection of our Lord Jesus Christ, who is now our High Priest. We are complete IN HIM.

After we are born of the Spirit and baptized with the Spirit we need the daily washing of the Word for our hands and our feet, which become defiled through contact with a sinful world. It is only as we walk in the light that the blood cleanses us from all sin.

The priests were washed or bathed all over, once, and for all. This sets forth our entire sanctification.

The priests, however, still needed a daily washing of their hands and feet, and this sets forth our constant need of atoning blood and the water of the Word to keep us clean after we are sanctified wholly.

THE CURTAINS

Moses was instructed to make "ten curtains of fine twined linen, and blue, and purple, and scarlet: with cherubim of cunning work"; He was also instructed to make "eleven curtains of goats' hair and a covering of rams' skins dyed red, and a covering above of badgers' skins." Thus was Moses commanded to make four different kinds of curtains in order to cover the sanctuary with its sacred furniture and vessels.

The first curtains of fine twined linen, and blue, and purple, and scarlet, set forth the heavenly, kingly, holy, and sacrificial life of Christ.

The second curtains of goats' hair set forth the separated one who was made a curse for us.

The third covering of rams' skins dyed red sets forth the suffering and agonies of Christ as our substitute.

The fourth curtain or covering of badgers' skins set forth the outward life of Christ as He walked amongst men.

It is of interest to note that the beautiful curtains could only be seen by those who entered the presence of God in the holy of holies. It is still true that the beauties of Christ are only to be seen from the *inside,* or after we are sanctified wholly. Everyone could see the common, rough badgers' skins, but we must step inside, past the veil, and into the holy of holies in order to behold the beauty of Christ.

THE BOARDS FOR THE TABERNACLE

Moses was commanded to make boards for the tabernacle of shittim wood standing up. Two tenons were to be made in one board and set in order one against another. The boards were to rest on forty sockets of silver and were kept together by ten bars also made of wood. In the midst of the boards there was to be a middle bar reaching from end to end. Both the boards and the bars were to be overlaid with gold.

The BOARDS for the tabernacle were a type of individual believers. They were to be standing up, *not* lying down. Stand. Stand upright. Having done all, stand. The boards also were to be united and kept together. Selah.

The boards were to stand on sockets of silver. SILVER in the Bible speaks of redemption. The boards were not resting upon the desert sands, but in sockets of silver. Believers are resting upon the redemption that is in Christ Jesus. The middle bar which was unseen by mortal eye and kept all the individual boards in their place sets forth the Holy Spirit, who, although unseen, keeps all individual believers standing upright in their place.

The ancient tabernacle in the wilderness, constructed and set up "as the Lord commanded Moses" (Exod. 11: 16-19), thus was a wonderful type of Christ and of all who are "in Him," saved by grace. Its foundation was silver, which silver was the ransom money paid by every Israelite (Exod. 30: 12-16). Part of this silver was made into sockets, which served as foundations, upon which the structure stood, firm and secure. This silver is typical of "the precious blood of Christ" (1 Pet. 1: 19), the true redemption price paid on Calvary.

The Boards, 48 in number, were of shittim wood, cut down from trees found in the desert, of little value in themselves, but each board stood on two tenons of silver valued at about $500 each. And these boards were all overlaid, actually encased, in pure gold. And thus it is, that every sinner believing in the Lord Jesus Christ, stands ON His work, and is accepted IN Himself.

Five Bars, bound all the boards together. Four outwardly passed through rings of gold. These were visible; one—"the middle bar"—passed through "the midst of the boards." It could not be seen, yet bound them all "in one," in a unity that could not be broken. And thus it is, that all true Christians have Christ IN them, forming them into "one" (Heb. 11: 11). Thus in "one Spirit they form one body" and are one in life with Christ and with each other. And "in one Spirit" all true saints are one.

Rings of gold are emblematic of that love which is in "the hearts" (Rom. 5: 5) of all born again people, and comes out in visible action (1 John 3: 18). And as these rings encircled the four bars and pressed them to their center, so always does real love in the saved, clasp the truth of God, and cause fellow-believers to cleave to Christ the center, to His truth and to those who are His.

The Silver Sockets of Redemption and Resurrection, on which the boards stood, were a permanent foundation which could not be shaken. And such is the Death and Resurrection of Christ, to all who build thereon. No storm can shake, no enemy destroy that foundation. Make sure you build for eternity there, and that you can truthfully say—

> "On Christ, the solid Rock, I stand,
> All other ground is sinking sand."

Two Tenons or hands (as the Bible margin names them, (Exod. 26: 17) on each board, took hold of the silver foundation, as faith in a sinner lays hold on Christ, and that moment stands "in Him" (Rom. 8: 1). The board was only a piece of common wood, of little value, estimated at about half a dollar, but the foundation upon which it stood was worth $500 in silver, and the "pure gold" with which it was covered, was of untold value. So in these boards and bars we have the great gospel truths of Christ UNDER all believing souls, Christ ON them, their acceptance before God, they IN Christ, raised up in Him, and Christ IN them, their bond of unity and their hope of glory (Col. 1: 27). The teacher has here a fine subject for a simple gospel talk, and a theme for "a word in season" to all who believe and are "in Christ." It is such simple, elementary fundamental truths, clearly taught from the Word and ministered in the grace and power of the spirit, that establish those who believe the Gospel and lead on in the ways that be in Christ, such as are truly "IN Christ Jesus."

THE VAIL

Moses was commanded to make a vail of blue, purple, and scarlet, and fine twined linen of cunning work. The vail was to hang upon four pillars of wood overlaid with gold. The vail was to separate the holy place from the most holy place. The *VAIL* speaks of the body of Christ. The blue, sets forth the heavenly Christ; the purple sets forth the kingly Christ; the scarlet sets forth the suffering Christ; and the fine twined linen of cunning work sets forth the holy life of Christ. The four pillars speak to us of the four gospels which set forth and support the heavenly, kingly, suffering, holy Christ. As the body of Christ was rent so the vail was rent from the top to the bottom.

When Jesus was dying on the cross of Calvary the priest was just about to enter the most holy place, and, as the Roman soldier pierced the side of Christ, the vail of the temple was rent in twain. This must have been one of the reasons why many of the priests believed in Christ. That vail was a type of the body of Christ: "The vail which is His body." It is now our privilege to enter into the holy of holies by this new and living way. Selah!

THE URIM AND THE THUMMIM

The Lord commanded Moses to take Aaron and his sons from among the children of Israel that they might minister unto the Lord in the priest's office. God also instructed him to make holy garments for Aaron for glory and for beauty.

There were seven articles of dress:

1. A Breastplate.
2. An Ephod.

3. A Robe.
4. An Embroidered Coat.
5. A Mitre or Crown.
6. A Girdle.
7. Linen Breeches.

The priests were perfectly clothed because seven is the number of perfection. These garments were to be made of gold, blue, purple, scarlet, and fine linen. Moses was also commanded to take two onyx stones and grave on them the names of the children of Israel, six of their names on one stone, and six names on the other stone, according to their birth. The engraver was to work the names in the stones like the engravings of a signet. The names were to be set in ouches of gold. Aaron was to bear these stones as stones of memorial.

The breast plate of judgment was to be made four square and was to be set with stones. Aaron was to bear upon his heart as he went into the holy place the names of the children of Israel in the breast plate of judgment. The Urim and the Thummim were put in the breastplate of judgment; thus Aaron was to bear the judgment of Israel upon his heart before the Lord continually.

The robe of the Ephod was to be a seamless garment made of blue. Upon the hem of the robe there were pomegranates of blue, purple and scarlet, and there were bells of gold between the pomegranates. As Aaron was ministering to the Lord the tinkling bells assured all who were interested that their priest was yet alive.

A plate of pure gold, with "Holiness to the Lord" engraved upon it, was also to be made and put upon the Mitre or Crown, which was put upon Aaron's forehead that he might bear the iniquity of the holy things and that Israel might be accepted before the Lord.

For Aaron's sons there were to be made coats, girdles, and bonnets for glory and for beauty. The sons were to be anointed, consecrated, and sanctified to minister unto the Lord in the priest's office.

Aaron sets forth our Lord Jesus Christ as our High Priest, while Aaron's sons set forth all true, regenerated believers, who are not only sons but also priests of the Lord. The gold, blue, purple, scarlet, and fine linen sets forth the heavenly and beautiful Christ, while the stones with the names of the children of Israel engraved upon them set forth the fact that Christ has us on His heart. As the stones were borne upon the shoulders and carried next to the heart, so Christ bears us on His shoulders and has us upon His heart.

The shoulder speaks of strength, the forehead speaks of remembrance, the bosom speaks of rest, and the heart speaks of affection and love.

The Urim and the Thummim, which means light and perfection, was the Divine method whereby Israel might know God's will. Our Urim and Thummim is the Holy Spirit and the Word of God. The Pomegranates speak of Divine fruitfulness; the bells of gold speak of divine testimony. The fruitful and faithful witness is none other than our Lord Jesus Christ. We, also, as priests, must have the golden bell of testimony and the pomegranates of fruitfulness in order that we die not.

Holiness unto the Lord is to be over and upon every thing that we do or say or think.

The linen breeches speak of the necessity of walking even as He walked. We also must be anointed, consecrated, and sanctified in order to minister in the priest's office.

10

THE SANCTIFICATION OF THE PRIESTS

The priests of the Lord, having already been called and chosen, are now about to be commissioned or ordained. Moses was commanded to take one young bullock, two rams without blemish, unleavened bread, cakes mingled with oil, and wafers anointed with oil, and to put all these in one basket, which was to be brought to the door of the tabernacle of the congregation by Aaron and his sons.

Aaron and his sons were to be washed with water, and then clothed with the beautiful garments and girded with the curious girdle of the Ephod. Then the mitre, together with the holy crown, was to be placed upon the head of Aaron. Moses was then to take the anointing oil and pour it upon Aaron's head and anoint him. Then Aaron's sons were to be brought, and, after being clothed, they were consecrated to the priest's office. Aaron and his sons were to place their hands upon the head of the ram which was to be killed. The tip of the right ear, the thumb of the right hand, and the great toe of the right foot of both Aaron and his sons, were sprinkled with the blood of the slain ram. Then they were to be anointed with oil. Having been consecrated and sanctified in this manner, they were to minister unto the Lord.

The Bullock sets forth our Lord Jesus Christ as the Servant of God and man.

The Ram speaks of Christ as the substitute for man.

The unleavened bread speaks of the Bread of Life, Christ, the separated and holy one.

The sons of Aaron were first washed with water and then anointed with oil. The washing of water speaks of our regeneration; the anointing or pouring with oil speaks of our entire sanctification. In this way we follow Christ, who was not only born of the Spirit, but also filled with the Spirit and led of the Spirit. After the washing of water (Regeneration), and after the anointing with oil (Entire Sanctification), we are then girded for service (Girdles), after which we walk in submissive obedience to God (Bonnets).

There is a very interesting and instructive meaning to the bonnets as there is to all else in these wonderful chapters. The covering for the head is a sign of subjection and submission. The bonnets worn by the priests were a sign of their subjection and submission first to Aaron, and then to God.

The High Priest came between God and man. He must be holy and free from all bodily infirmities. He was washed with water, anointed with oil, clothed with garments of glory and beauty, and girded for holy service. He wore a mitre and a crown with these words of fire, "Holiness to the Lord," written across the mitre. He made intercession as well as atonement for the children of Israel. After going into the presence of God and making atonement, he came out and blessed the people, and the people shouted.

There was no other way of approach to God except through the High Priest. He was alone in his order, for there were no higher priests or highest priests. He was anointed in a very special way. He announced the will of God to men by the Urim and Thummim. He consecrated and initiated priests, presided over all sacred conventions, and directed in all matters of religion. He was to be above all natural and human affection and grief. He could marry only a pure virgin. Apart from him there was no salvation for either Jews or Gentiles.

The High Priest was a striking type of Christ. Holy, harmless, undefiled, separate from sinners, free from bodily infirmities, baptized with water by John, and anointed by the Spirit, He made an atonement for all. He is now in the presence of God making intercession for us. There is no other way of approach to God, for there is none other name given under heaven among men whereby we must be saved. There is none higher. He is the President and Director in all matters of true religion and announces to His people the will and Word of God. He who is *now* in the presence of God shall come again to rapture and bless His people.

OIL
(Type of the Holy Spirit)

1. Oil in the Candlestick:
   The Holy Spirit filling the Church.
2. Oil in the Branches:
   The Holy Spirit filling individual believers.
3. Oil in a Cruse:
   The Holy Spirit possessing our bodies, i. e., vessels of clay.
4. Oil on the Ear (quick to hear).
5. Oil on the Hand (Holy Service).
6. Oil on the Foot (Holy Walk).
7. Oil on the Head (Holy Wisdom).

"The Bible is like a wide and beautiful landscape seen afar off, dim and confused; but a good telescope will bring it near, and spread out all its rocks, and trees, and flowers, and verdant fields, and winding rivers at one's very feet. That telescope is the Spirit's teaching."—Dr. Thomas Chalmers.

11

THE PRINCIPAL SPICES

Moses was commanded to take principal spices of pure myrrh, sweet cinnamon, sweet calamus, cassia, and olive oil, and make an oil of holy ointment, which should be an holy anointing oil.

He was also instructed to take the sweet spices, stacte, onycha, and galbanum, with pure frankincense and make a perfume tempered perfectly together, pure and holy. Some of these sweet spices were to be beaten very small and placed before the testimony in the tabernacle of the congregation, where God promised to meet with His people. Imitation of his anointing oil and holy perfume was forbidden under penalty of death. All these things are of interest to us in this present dispensation.

1. Myrrh. Myrrh is obtained from a tree by means of incisions. It is a bitter gum which spontaneously flows from the tree, and which is used as a medicine to ease pain. Christ was wounded for our transgressions and bruised for our iniquities. He tasted the bitter cup for us. Through His sufferings and the incisions caused by the nails driven in His hands and feet, He has become our Myrrh. "By His stripes we are healed."

2. Sweet Cinnamon. Sweet cinnamon is obtained from the bark of a small evergreen tree such as is found in places like Ceylon. While travelling from Japan to Marseilles of France we stopped at Ceylon and tasted of the bark of these cinnamon trees. Sweet cinnamon is used for

flavoring, is sweet and agreeable, and is a stimulant and also a cordial. Its shoots stand erect. It is HOT AND SWEET. Selah!

These qualities are all found in Jesus Christ, and, when He anoints us with the holy anointing oil of the Spirit, these qualities will also be seen in us. It is possible to be HOT and at the same time to be SWEET. A cordial brings *cheer*, a stimulant brings *encouragement*, and the erect shoots remind us that we should walk uprightly.

3. Sweet Calamus. The one beautiful thing about the sweet calamus is that its fragrance is brought out by crushing. The more it is crushed and the harder it is beaten, the more fragrance it yields. It also grows erect.

   Sweet Calamus speaks of our Lord Jesus Christ sending up the sweet fragrance of a sweet, holy life to God. The more He was beaten and the more He was trampled upon, the more fragrance went up to God as a sweet smelling savor.

4. Cassia. The bark of the Cassia tree is removed by scraping. It is used as a medicine and as a flavoring. Although it is bitter to the taste, it is noted for its great soothing qualities.

All these spices were blended and mixed together to make an holy anointing oil. They set forth the sweetness and power of our Lord Jesus Christ, the Anointer with the Spirit. The bitter taste in some of these spices sets forth the sufferings and death of Christ.

The holy anointing oil was not put upon a stranger; hence the anointing is not for sinners. It was not put upon the flesh; hence there is no such thing as being anointed or being filled with the Spirit on top of the Old Man. The holy anointing oil was put upon people consecrated for service.

The sweet spices also have a meaning for us today:

1. Stacte. This is also obtained from a tree by incisions. The gum drops from the tree like drops of rain coming from the heavens. The word Stacte means *to drop* or *distill*. When trampled upon Stacte yields its fragrance. This is true of Christ, and ought to be true with all believers.

2. Onycha. This is obtained from a shell fish found in the Red Sea, which, when it is crushed, yields a sweet smelling perfume. It also has healing qualities and is beneficial to man. It is fragrant to God and healing to man. This is all true of our Lord Jesus Christ (1) Fragrant to God, (2) Healing to man.

3. Galbanum. This word means to be fat or fertile and refers to the abundant sap of the plant. It is used to drive away vermin, reptiles, and pests.

4. Frankincense. This is a well known spice, which is obtained by incisions. It is very valuable, is an antidote to poison, and can live and grow in the hardest places. It even grows upon bare rocks.

There are sermons in all these words, and, taken together, they set forth the fragrance of Christ's life and lips. Crushed in death, He yielded an holy perfume to God and purchased health, help, and holiness for man. The Holy energy which burned in His righteous soul drives away all reptiles and poisons and rebukes all half hearted service. These spices set forth the spotless purity of Him who came to destroy the works of the Devil. He can drive carnality from the heart and chase the vermin of hell from the soul. He can fill us with His own presence and power and make us more than conquerors. Bless His holy name.

The sweet spices — stacte, onycha, galbanum, and pure frankincense—all evenly mixed made a pure and holy perfume.

These different ingredients were to be beaten very small and then placed on a brazen altar in the holiest of all.

All this speaks of Christ. Christ is not only our Lamb slain, our Shepherd Guide, our Ark, our Ram, our Pillar of Fire, our Tree cut down, our Bread and Water of Life, our Substitute, our Captain, our Great High Priest, our Bullock, our Goat, our Dove, our Offering, our Rock, our Savior, and our Coming King; He is our All in All. He is our Holy Perfume.

The pounding and beating of these special spices into small pieces shadow the intense sufferings of Christ; through His offering, His sufferings, His sacrifices, and His intercession we have access unto the Father. We present the Holy perfume of the spotless, sacrificial, sweet, HOLY, pure life of Christ and are accepted in the Beloved. No imitation or comparison was to be made, for Christ cannot be imitated and Christ cannot be compared. Buddha, Confucius, Russell, Eddy, Smith, White, Krishnamurti, or Mohammed are all in a different class. There can be no comparison. The study of comparative religions does not include Christianity. Christianity stands by itself. Buddha's perfume, like Russell's prayers and Mohammed's curses, get no higher than the ceiling.

No life or prayer or work can ever rise into the nostrils of God without Christ being All in All.

God cannot accept anything nor any one outside of Christ.

All, whether infant, or adult, rich or poor, saint or sinner, wise or ignorant, English or Hottentot, are doomed outside of Christ.

12

THE ANOINTING OF THE SPIRIT

The Holy Spirit is the third person of the ever blessed Trinity, and, in this age or dispensation, He is the executive of the Godhead. This age in which we live is distinctively the age or dispensation of the Spirit.

The Holy Spirit has always been an active agent in the Universe. He is seen in the first verse of the Bible: "In the beginning God." The word for God here is in the plural and implies God the Father, God the Son, and God the Holy Ghost.

The Holy Spirit was thus an active agent in the work of Creation.

The second reference to the Holy Spirit is in the second verse where we find the Spirit of God moving upon the darkness of a ruined world: "The Spirit of God moved upon the face of the waters." The picture is that of a hen sitting on eggs or of a dove sitting on its nest patiently waiting to bring forth life. The Holy Ghost brooded over the darkness until light and life appear. This is the office of the Spirit. He moves or broods over the darkness of man's soul seeking to bring forth life and light.

The next reference to the Holy Spirit is in connection with Noah and the Ark.

The dove was sent forth three times. The first time it returned, having found no place to rest. The second time it returned with an olive branch which it had plucked. The third time it returned no more unto the ark.

The Ark is a type of Christ; the dove is a beautiful type of the Spirit.

At his first coming he found no place to rest. At his second appearing the olive branch of peace was with him.

At his third coming he came to abide forever. The first coming sets forth his Old Testament activities. He was unable to find an abiding place. He came the second time as a dove, resting on the prince of peace. The third coming was on the Day of Pentecost when he came to abide.

The raven was a type of Satan, who could rest and find satisfaction amidst the ruins of a sinful world.

The dove which was a type of the Spirit could find no rest until he came to abide in the hearts of redeemed men.

The Holy Spirit is next seen in the twenty-fourth chapter of Genesis in the person of Eliezer, the servant of Abraham and Isaac.

Abraham is a type of God the Father, while Isaac is a type of God the Son, and Eliezer is a type of the Spirit seeking to win a bride for the father's well beloved son.

Eliezer was the eldest servant of the loving Father and ruled over all that Abraham had. He was to go to the household of Abraham in order to seek and win a bride for the obedient son, Isaac. He was *not to compel but* WIN a bride for the son of the loving father.

Eliezer took ten camels and departed. All the goods of his master were in his hands. He made his camels to kneel down by a well of water outside of the city. It was the time of evening and it came to pass that Rebekah, with her pitcher upon her shoulder, came out to the well. She was a very beautiful maiden, a virgin, and a willing, untiring worker. As soon as Rebekah satisfied the requirements of this winner of souls, Eliezer took a golden earring and two bracelets and gave them to the prospective bride.

He was invited home where a welcome awaited him and where meat was set before him. He refused to eat, however, until he had told his errand. Eliezer never spoke of himself, but always of the father and son. He honored the father and the son. He magnified the father and the son. He made known his mission and demanded an immediate answer one way or the other. Having accomplished his purpose he sat down and enjoyed the fellowship of the qualifying bride. He also brought forth jewels of silver and jewels of gold and raiment and gave them to Rebekah. He gave also to her brother and to her mother precious things. They then ate and drank. After spending the night with Bethuel and his household, Eliezer departed the next morning with his captured bride. He guided her safely into the arms of her loving Isaac and the bell rings down the curtain with Isaac and Rebekah taking a honeymoon trip to his father's house. How wonderful is the word of God.

Eliezer is a type of the Spirit. He, as the executive of the Godhead in this age, rules over all. He is seeking to win a bride for Christ. The bride is not to be compelled but wooed and won. All the possessions of the loving Father and obedient Son are in his hands. It is evening time. The morning has passed and gone. The sun is setting. The darkness is coming on. He watches and waits at the well of water, which is THE WORD. He bestows the proofs of acceptance on the one who qualifies. His zeal knows no bounds. He never speaks of himself, and he perseveres until he wins the bride and escorts her safely to the home and heart of the happy bridegroom. We must follow the Holy Spirit if we wish to become the bride.

Another beautiful type of the Spirit is seen in the story of Joseph's steward.

Joseph had been falsely accused, misrepresented, maligned, misunderstood, and rejected. In order to bring his brethren to realize their wrongs, he sends his steward after them, and, when they acknowledge their guilt and are truly humbled and at their wit's end, Joseph finally reveals himself to them.

Joseph is a beautiful type of Christ and Joseph's servant is a beautiful type of the Spirit convicting of sin, righteousness, and judgment and bringing men to a state and place where they may be reconciled to Christ.

After Israel had been delivered from Egypt and had crossed the Red Sea, they found themselves without any water. Moses approached a rock, smote it, and forthwith, the rock gave forth its water.

The Rock is Christ. The smitten rock is the crucified Christ. The water is the Spirit who was given after the rock was smitten.

The Holy Spirit can also be seen in type by the oil in the Candlestick.

The candlestick is a type of Christ and the Church.

The Oil is a type of the Spirit. Christ was filled with the Spirit, hence was the light of the world. Believers must be filled with the Spirit for "Ye are the light of the world."

The oil in the candlestick was unseen, but, nevertheless, it was a glorious reality, giving light to all in the Holy place. In some of the offerings oil was mingled or poured or anointed; all these things beautifully reveal the work of the Holy Spirit.

The meal was a type of Christ. Meal, mingled with oil, speaks of Christ conceived and born of the Spirit.

Oil poured or anointed speaks of Christ being anointed by the Spirit for his service and sacrifice.

In fact, to those who have eyes to see and ears to hear, the Bible is filled with types of Christ and the Holy Spirit.

The middle bar of the Old Testament Tabernacle, which kept each of the upright boards in its place, is a wonderful type of the Holy Spirit.

Joshua, the leader of Israel's hosts, bringing them into their promised possessions, is a beautiful type of the Holy Spirit. It was expedient for Israel that Moses go away for if Moses go not away their Joshua could not come.

Joshua with his sword is a type of the Holy Spirit and the Word.

Bezaleel is another great type of the Spirit, the Master Workman.

Elisha is also a foreshadowing of the Holy Spirit. Elijah was taken up into heaven and Elisha begins his ministry.

At last the day of Pentecost dawns and the Holy Spirit dispensation is ushered in. Now sinners may be born of the Spirit and believers may be baptized with the Spirit. The Baptized may be anointed by the Spirit for special service for God, and all may enjoy the Witness of the Spirit both to their regeneration and entire sanctification, for the Spirit himself bears witness with our spirit that we are the children of God and the Holy Ghost has perfected for ever those who are sanctified, whereof the Holy Ghost also is a witness to us. Have you been born of the Spirit? Have you been baptized with the Spirit? Are you enjoying the witness of the Spirit? Are you living under the constant anointing of the Holy Spirit?

13

CHRIST IN ALL THE SCRIPTURES

Christ fills the Word of God. He is the seed of the woman in Genesis and the Passover lamb in Exodus. He is the High Priest of Leviticus and the uplifted one in Numbers as well as the star of Jacob. He is the Prophet like unto Moses in Deuteronomy and Captain of the Lord's host in Joshua. He is the righteous Judge and deliverer and also the messenger of Jehovah in Judges. He is the Kinsmen-redeemer-Bridegroom of Ruth and the Lord of David in Samuel. He is the King of Kings of the book of Kings and Chronicles. He is the restorer of his people in Ezra and Nehemiah as well as Lord of heaven and earth. He is the Mordecai of Esther working in secret on behalf of the people of God and woe to the Hamans who seek the hurt of God's people. He is the Redeemer of Job. He is the Blessed Man of Psalm 1 and the Blessed King of Psalm 2 as he is the Man of Sorrows of Psalm 3 and so on ad-infinitum.

He is the One above the Sun in Ecclesiastes as He is the Wisdom of God in Proverbs. He is the Lily of the Valley, the Rose of Sharon and the chiefest among ten thousand in the Song of Songs.

He is the suffering Servant, Lord, and Prophet of Isaiah. He is the Lord of Righteousness in Jeremiah. He is the Jehovah Jireh and Jehovah Mekkaddeshcem of Ezekiel as He is the Messiah and Smiting Stone of Daniel. He fills the historical books as He fills the Pentateuch. He fills the minor Prophecies as He fills the Major Prophecies.

He is the One who pours out the Holy Spirit in Joel. He is the Desire of All Nations in Haggai, as He is the Sun of Righteousness in Malachi.

He is the King of the Jews in Matthew and the Servant of Jehovah in Mark. He is the Perfect Man in Luke as He is the Son of God in John. He is the Ascended Lord and Christ in Acts as He is the Lord of Righteousness in Romans. He is the First-fruits of them that slept in Corinthians and the Fulfiller of the Law in Galatians. He is the Head over all things to His body, the Church, in Ephesians and He is the fulness of the Godhead bodily in Colossians. He is the Coming One in Thessalonians as He is the Sanctifier and Interceder of Hebrews. He is the Lamb upon the Throne and rightful claimant to the New Heavens and New Earth and New City. He is Earth's rightful Lord of Lords and King of Kings.

He is our Second Man and last Adam. He is our Substitute, Seth, as He is our dying Enos. He is our purchasing Canaan as well as our rising and glorified Mahalaleel. He is our Jared and Enoch and Conquering Lamech giving us our REST(Noah).

He is our Reuben (Son), our Simeon (listening), our Levi (Joined), our Judah (lion of praise). He is our Zebulun and Issachar as He is our Dan (Judge). He is our Wrestler (Naphtali) as He is our Joseph and Benjamin, the son of the Father's Right Hand. He is our Isaac, offered, and our Jacob, Prince with God.

He is our Passover and Tabernacle, the dwelling place of God and meeting place between God and Man. He is All and in All.

14

GOD'S MINISTERS

"And the Lord spake unto Moses, saying, See, I have called by name Bezaleel the son of Uri, the son of Hur, of the tribe of Judah: And I have filled him with the spirit of God, in wisdom, and in understanding, and in knowledge, and in all manner of workmanship. And I, behold, I have given with him Aholiab the son of Ahisamach, of the tribe of Dan: and in the hearts of all that are wise-hearted I have put wisdom, that they may make all that I have commanded thee" (Ex. 31: 1-6).

There were two men who were especially called and equipped by God to make the Tabernacle.

1. Bezaleel.

>   Bezaleel was the son of Uri who was of Hur, of the tribe of Judah.

2. Aholiab.

>   Aholiab was the son of Ahisamach, of the tribe of Dan.

All names of persons, places, and things have their special instruction and interest for us today. These seven names and their meaning illustrate the Minister's secret of success in his work for God and souls.

Seven is the number which sets forth *perfection* and typifies the perfect workmen in the Divine sense. Taking them in their order as they appear in the above scripture we have:

1. Bezaleel.

>   Bezaleel means *in the shadow of God*. Here is the first secret of success in the work of the Lord. "He that dwelleth in the secret place of the most high" is the one in the shadow of God's Presence. God is within speaking distance of His shadow.

2. Uri.

> Uri means "Light of Jehovah." The faithful and successful minister will live in the light of Jehovah. Day after day finds him walking in the light. He walks in the light of God's Holy Word instead of in the ungodly counsels of the unsanctified. He walks in the light of God's Presence and power and knows no defeat.

3. Hur.

> The word Hur is a very remarkable word. With only three letters it also has three meanings. It means:
> 1. To be *free-born*.
> 2. To be *noble*.
> 3. To be *white*.
>
> Hur represents those who are born again of the Spirit of God for those are the truly free born ones. They are among the nobility of the skies. They keep themselves and their garments white and unspotted from the world. They are free-born, noble, and white.

4. Judah.

> Judah means *Praise*.
>
> Here is one of the secrets of a successful ministry. Here is the spirit of buoyancy and optimism. Here is the thankful, joyful spirit, and a certain harbinger of spiritual success in soul saving.

5. Aholiab.

> Aholiab means *tent of my father*.
>
> A tent, in Bible terms, speaks of *Separation*. Separation from sin and the world. A tent-dweller is a person who is traveling, wandering; he is ready to move at a moment's notice and by living in a tent he confesses to being a pilgrim and a stranger on the earth. His citizenship is in heaven, and he is

constantly in readiness for his journey to his happy homeland above.

Aholiab would remind the preacher that he is a pilgrim and a stranger here and that heaven is his home.

6. Ahisamach.

This name is made up of two words; one of which means *support* and the other to be *brotherly*. Hence it means *brotherly support*.

Ahisamach strikes a death blow to all the bickerings, jealousies, wire pullings, and politics indulged in by professional preachers. The Baptism with the Holy Spirit is a unifying baptism.

7. Dan.

Dan means "to judge."

When Dan was born the mother said, "Now hath the Lord judged me," and the baby was named Dan. Our sins were judged on the cross. We shall stand before the judgment seat of Christ to be judged for reward. We are now to judge ourselves, take an inventory of ourselves and judge or take sides against ourselves. We are not to be judges of others, but judges of our selves. Here are seven secrets of the successful soul winner. He lives in the shadow of God; walks in the light; having been free born, he keeps himself unspotted from the world; lives a life of praise, thanksgiving and devotion to God; is happy to acknowledge himself a pilgrim and a stranger here; and with a spirit of brotherly love and oneness he judges himself and leaves his brethren in the hands of the Lord, working with them and loving them with a pure heart fervently. This is the story of God's Workmen as recorded in Ex. 31: 1-6.

15

SYNTHETIC STUDY OF EXODUS

The Grand subject of Exodus is that of Redemption. In Genesis we have *creation* and fall, and the announcement of a deliverer in the seed of the woman (the God man); while in Exodus we have *redemption* through the shed blood of the Passover lamb. There is undoubtedly a reason for the picture of the People of God in Egypt being shown to us at the opening of Exodus. In the Scripture Egypt is a type of the world.

The opening chapters of Exodus reveal to us:

(1) The utter impotence of the enemy to frustrate the purposes of God. The Mightiest Monarch in the world is powerless against God and powerless against the people of God.

(2) The fear of God can lift the feeblest and humblest above the fear of man. Shiphrah and Puah "did not as the king commanded."

(3) The impossibility of defeating the plans and purposes of God.

The best commentary on Exodus 2 is the eleventh chapter of Hebrews. Exodus is a simple record of the human side; while Hebrews gives the divine side. The king had commanded that every son born should be cast into the river. The inexorable decree of the despotic king stood between the birth and continued life of Moses and the plans of God, but *"By faith Moses . . . was hid."* They owed allegiance to their earthly sovereign, but they owed allegiance to the Lord of Lords first.

3. The Commission of Moses . . . . Chapters 3-4.

Forty is the number of probation, the time of testing, and hence Moses must need spend his first forty years in the Palace, and his next forty years in the desert before the last forty years of his life can be spent leading the people of God from Egypt to Canaan.

"Now Moses kept the flock of Jethro his father-in-law, the priest of Midian: and he led the flock to the back side of the desert, and came to the mountain of God, even to Horeb. And the angel of the Lord appeared unto him in a flame of fire out of the midst of a bush: and he looked, and, behold, the bush burned with fire, and the bush was not consumed" (Ex. 3: 1, 2).

It is most interesting to trace the appearings of God to his people in the Old Testament. There are three parts to this vision of Exodus 3: 1, 2:

(1) The Lord.
(2) The Fire.
(3) The Bush.

These are all Old Testament foreshadowings of our Lord Jesus Christ. The bush represented the Children of Israel. There is nothing more easily consumed by fire than a bush; and it was chosen on this very account to foreshadow the nation of Israel in the furnace of Egypt, the fire burning, purifying, cleansing, but not destroying it.

It is instructive to outline the series of difficulties raised by Moses.

(1) "And Moses said unto God, Who am I, that I should go unto Pharaoh, and that I should bring forth the children of Israel out of Egypt" (Ex. 3: 11).

(2) "And Moses said unto God, behold, when I come unto the children of Israel, and shall say unto them, The God of your fathers hath sent me unto you; and they shall say to me, What is his name? what shall I say unto them?" (Ex. 3: 13).

(3) "And Moses answered and said, But, behold, they will not believe me, nor hearken unto my voice; for they will say, The Lord hath not appeared unto thee" (Ex. 4: 1).

(4) "And Moses said unto the Lord, O my Lord, I am not eloquent, neither heretofore, nor since thou hast spoken unto thy servant; but I am slow of speech, and of a slow tongue" (Ex. 4: 10).

(5) "And he said, O my Lord, send, I pray thee, by the hand of him whom thou wilt send" (Ex. 4: 13).

4. The first message to Pharaoh ....Chapters 5, 6.

"And afterward Moses and Aaron went in, and told Pharaoh, Thus saith the Lord God of Israel, Let my people go, that they may hold a feast unto me in the wilderness. And Pharaoh said, Who is the Lord, that I should obey his voice to let Israel go? I know not the Lord, neither will I let Israel go. And they said, The God of the Hebrews hath met with us: let us go, we pray thee, three days' journey into the desert, and sacrifice unto the Lord our God; lest he fall upon us with pestilence, or with the sword. And the king of Egypt said unto them, Wherefore do ye, Moses and Aaron, let the people from their works? get you unto your burdens. And Pharaoh said, Behold, the people of the land now are many, and ye make them rest from their burdens" (Exodus 5: 1-5).

Pharaoh, as the god of the world—Satan, holds the people in bondage. God's purpose is one of deliverance for His own joy and glory, their good, and the world's future blessing. Pharaoh placed himself in direct and complete antagonism with God. This antagonism continued until Pharaoh was destroyed.

5. Judgments upon Egypt ....Chapters 7-11.
   God himself takes issue against Pharaoh and a succession of terrible judgments fall upon Pharaoh and Egypt.
   (1) The waters of the Nile are turned into blood.
   (2) The plague of frogs.
   (3) Lice.
   (4) Swarms of flies.
   (5) Murrain upon cattle.
   (6) Boils.
   (7) Thunder and hail.
   (8) Locusts.
   (9) Darkness.
   (10) Death.

6. The Passover ....Chapters 12-15.
   The great difference between Egypt and Israel lay not in any moral superiority of Israel over Egypt, but wholly, solely, and entirely in *the blood of the*

Paschal Lamb. It was in the blood of the innocent lamb that righteousness and peace kissed each other, and mercy and truth met together.

7. The Song of Redemption ....Chapter 15.
This song is twofold: (1) It applies to Israel and (2) It is typical of the believer. There is no singing mentioned in the Bible except in connection with redemption. Angels do not sing. As far as the Bible is concerned, angels have never sung since sin entered the universe of God. Israel, as a redeemed people laden with the joy of their Lord, tell it out in such accents of gratitude and praise as are set forth in this inspiring song.

8. Marah and Elim ....Chapter 15: 22-27.
The strains of Israel's songs had scarcely died away before their pilgrim journey is commenced. "So Moses brought Israel from the Red Sea; and they went out into the wilderness of Shur; and they went three days' journey into the wilderness, and found no water. And when they came to Marah, they could not drink of the waters of Marah for they were bitter: therefore the name of it was called Marah. And the people murmured against Moses, saying, What shall we drink? And he cried unto the Lord; and the Lord shewed him a tree, which when he had cast into the waters, the waters were made sweet: there he made for them a statute and an ordinance, and there he proved them, and said, If thou wilt diligently hearken to the voice of the Lord thy God, and wilt do that which is right in his sight, and wilt give ear to his commandments, and keep all his statutes, I will put none of these diseases upon thee,

which I have brought upon the Egyptians: for I am the Lord that healeth thee. And they came to Elim, where were twelve wells of water, and threescore and ten palm trees; and they encamped there by the waters" (Exodus 15: 22-27).

9. Manna ....Chapter 16.
"This is the bread which the Lord hath given you to eat" (Ex. 16: 13-21).
"The bread of God is He which cometh down from heaven and giveth life unto the world" (John 6: 32, 33).

10. Rephidim and Amalek ....Chapter 17.
"All these things happened unto them for types"; and, "They are written for our admonition" (1 Cor. 10: 11.
The manna sets forth Christ as the bread of God. The smitten rock foreshadows Christ crucified. The gushing water from the rock typifies the Holy Spirit. "Whosoever drinketh of the water that I shall give him shall never thirst but the water that I shall give him shall be IN HIM a well of water springing up into everlasting life."
Immediately after the waters gushed from the smitten rock there is revealed a desperate conflict with Amalek. If Pharaoh is unable to keep Israel in Egypt Amalek will seek to kill them before they enter Canaan.
The manna is Christ come down from heaven; the smitten rock is Christ crucified; the living water is an emblem of the Holy Spirit, which we receive in regeneration, and immediately after the reception of the Spirit there is conflict. This must always be so for the flesh lusteth against the Spirit and the

Spirit against the flesh: and these are contrary one to the other.

The real character of Amalek may be apprehended by a study of his origin (see Gen. 36: 12).

"Who shall separate us from the love of Christ? . . . Nay in all these things we are more than conquerors" (Rom. 8: 34-37).

11. Sinai ....Chapters 18-20.

Jethro, the priest of Midian, brought Zipporah and her two sons to Moses. Moses, the Jew, declares to Jethro, the Gentile, all that the Lord had done. Jethro (the Gentile) then unites in worship with Aaron and the elders of Israel. Moses (Jews) and Jethro (Gentiles) eat bread together before God. Thus is foreshadowed the millennium and its blessings. Then comes Sinai with its law and the ushering in of a new dispensation.

There are several points in connection with Sinai which demand attention:

(1) The nature of the law.

The first four commandments relate to God and the last six to man. They thus define responsibility (1) towards God and (2) towards man.

(2) The object of the law:

The commandments were to prove Israel. Israel promised obedience and these commandments enabled them to judge themselves. The object of the law was NOT to give life or holiness, but as a test of Israel's allegiance.

(3) The effect of the law:

The people were terrified and they stood afar off. Sinners cannot stand in the presence of a righteous God. They are thus at a distance actually and morally, and only grace can bring us nigh. A mediator is thus required, and Moses sets forth Christ, who is the "one Mediator between God and men" (1 Tim. 2: 5).

12. The Statutes or Judgments ....Chapters 21-23.

God's care for His people is clearly revealed in the *judgments* or *statutes* which He gave to govern his people in their many and varied relationships.

(1) The Hebrew Servant in Exodus 21: 2-6:

"If thou buy an Hebrew servant, six years he shall serve; and in the seventh he shall go out free for nothing. If he came in by himself, he shall go out by himself: if he were married, then his wife shall go out with him. If his master have given him a wife, and she have borne him sons or daughters: the wife and her children shall be her master's, and he shall go out by himself. And if the servant shall plainly say, I love my master, my wife, and my children; I will not go out free: then his master shall bring him unto the judges; he shall also bring him to the door, or unto the door post; and his master shall bore his ear through with an awl; and he shall serve him for ever."

This Hebrew servant is a very beautiful type of Christ who (1) took upon himself the form of a servant; (2) came to do the will of God; (3) served and served perfectly His allotted time; and (4) could have claimed freedom.

Christ went to the cross (1) for the glory of God; (2) the salvation of man; (3) to obtain for Himself a church and (4) to obtain a bride.

Because Christ loved His master and loved His bride and loved his children, He would not go out free.

(2) The maidservant sold by her father:

"And if a man sell his daughter to be a maidservant, she shall not go out as the men-servants do. If she please not her master, who hath betrothed her to himself, then shall he let her be redeemed: to sell her unto a strange nation he shall have no power, seeing he hath dealt deceitfully with her. And if he hath betrothed her unto his son, he shall deal with her after the manner of daughters. If he take him another wife; her food, her raiment, and her duty of marriage, shall he not diminish. And if he do not these three unto her, then shall she go out free without money" (Exodus 21: 7-11).

In compassionate love Jehovah surrounds the weak and defenseless with laws in order to insure their equitable and considerate treatment. The maid was not to be at the mercy of the moods and caprice of her master. There must be justice, righteousness, and mercy in all dealings.

(3) Divers ordinances:

(1) The death penalty.
(2) Personal injury.
(3) Ownership and responsibility.
(4) The law of restitution.
(5) Respect for constituted authority.
(6) Sins of the tongue.
(7) The Sabbath.

13. The Tabernacle ....Chapters 25-27.

After the ratification of the covenant (Ex. 24) we enter upon a new subject. God seeks a closer walk with His people, and desires for His people a closer walk with Him; hence the Tabernacle.

"And the Lord spake unto Moses, saying, speak unto the children of Israel, that they bring me an offering: of every man that giveth it willingly with his heart he shall take my offering. And this is the offering which ye shall take of them; gold, and silver, and brass, and blue, and purple, and scarlet, and fine linen, and goats' hair, and rams' skins dyed red, and badgers' skins, and shittim wood, oil for the light, spices for anointing oil, and for sweet incense, onyx stones, and stones to be set in the ephod, and in the breastplate. And let them make me a sanctuary; that I may dwell among them. According to all that I shew thee, after the pattern of the tabernacle, and the pattern of all the instruments thereof, even so shall ye make it" (Ex. 25: 1-9).

14. The Priesthood ....Chapters 28-40.

"And take thou unto thee Aaron thy brother, and his sons with him, from among the children of Israel, that he may minister unto me in the priest's office, even Aaron, Nadab and Abihu, Eleazar and Ithamar, Aaron's sons" (Ex. 28: 1).

The necessity for the appointment of Priests lay in the fact that all were sinners. Sinners cannot approach God. The Priests were to act as ministers (1) unto God, (2) unto the people. Aaron therefore became a type of Christ and Aaron's sons became a type of the church or born again ones. The

Priests, their consecration to service, and their qualifications for service are all set forth in these closing chapters, which are full of interest and instruction for all God's people for all ages.

In the foregoing fourteen points we have a full outline of the second book of the Bible—the book of Exodus, the book of Redemption.

THE BIBLE IS—

The charter of all true liberty.
The forerunner of all civilization.
The molder of institutions and governments.
The fashion of law.
The secret of national progress.
The guide of history.
The ornament and mainspring of literature.
The inspiration of philosophies.
The text-book of ethics.
The light of the intellect.
The soul of all strong heart life.
The illuminator of darkness.
The foe of superstition.
The enemy of oppression.
The uprooter of sin.
The comfort in sorrow.
The strength in weakness.
The pathway in perplexity.
The escape from temptation.
The steadier in the day of power.
The embodiment of all lofty ideals.
The begetter of life.
The promise of the future.
The star of death's night.
The revealer of God.
The guide and the hope and the inspiration of man.—
BISHOP WM. F. ANDERSON.

PART II

POINTS FOR EMPHASIS

A PICTURE OF SLAVERY

(Exodus 1: 6-14)

The book of Exodus sets forth in type and shadow, the sinner's bondage and God's redemption. Israel, as slaves in Egypt, redeemed by the blood of the Lamb, delivered by the power of Jehovah, led through the wilderness, brought into Canaan—present, as in a living parable, a Divinely-written "Pilgrim's Progress," the sinner's history from slavery in sin, to freedom in grace and entrance on glory.

1. *Bitter Bondage.*—Israel is in bondage. Jacob's sons, who had gone down into the land of Goshen, seventy persons in all, had become a great nation, numbering over two million souls. After Joseph's death, another king arose who knew not Joseph, and became the oppressor of Israel. Pharaoh, the official name of Egypt's ruler, is here a type of Satan, the world's prince (John 12: 11-31), under whose power (Col. 1: 13) sinners are held (Luke 11: 21; Col. 1: 13) as the bondslaves of sin (Rom. 6: 22).

2. *Serving Egypt's Gods.*—They had forgotten the God of their fathers, and had become worshippers of the gods of Egypt (Josh. 24: 14). They evidently had "a good time" in Egypt during Joseph's life, but soon they learn, as all sinners must, that "the way of transgressors is hard," and the bitterness of those who forget God. All who serve the god of this age are idolators (2 Cor. 4: 4), and only when Christ is received in the heart, do these idols lose their power (1 Thess. 1: 9).

94

3. *Their Cry for Deliverance.*—In their distress they cry to God (chap. 11: 23). Helpless and "without strength" (Rom. 5: 6), their help must come from above. Thus it is that God delivers sinners still. He knows their need, has seen their sorrow, and is moved with compassion toward them. It was to express this compassion that He sent His Son to save (John 3: 17) sinners (1 Tim. 1: 15), and give deliverance (Luke 4: 18) to the captives.

Illustration.—Four men, entombed in a coal pit, sought a way of escape at each of its ends, then at both sides, but none was available. Baffled and without hope one said, "If we are to be delivered it must be from above." Their signal of distress brought the rescuing party DOWN, and they were taken up.

EGYPT
(Type of the World)

1. Condemned.
2. Ripening for judgment.
3. Place of bondage, slavery, oppression.
4. God's people taken out.
5. Overthrown.
6. Punished for its iniquity.

PHARAOH
(Type of Satan)

1. King of Egypt.
2. Hated and afflicted the people of God.
3. Murdered God's little ones.
4. Opposed the Will of God.
5. Hardened himself against God.
6. Rebelled against the commands of God.
7. Judgment was pronounced upon him.
8. Defied God.

9. He was punished.
10. Finally, he perished.

PHARAOH'S POLICY
(Type of Worldly, Satanic Policy)

1. Ever awake to selfish interests.
2. Imagining danger or loss to himself.
3. Ungrateful.
4. Regardless of the rights of others.
5. A Cruel despot.

ISRAEL'S BONDAGE

Israel's bondage in Egypt is a type of the sinner's bondage in sin. Egypt is a type of the world lying in the evil one. Pharaoh is a type of the devil. Christ is the great Emancipator.

Notice SEVEN Bible characters who were in bondage.

1. The Pharisee was in bondage to Self.

> "The Pharisee stood and prayed thus with himself, God, I thank thee, that I am not as other men are, extortioners, unjust, adulterers, or even as this publican" (Luke 18: 11).

2. Esau was in bondage to his Stomach.

> "And Esau said, Behold I am at the point to die; and what profit shall this birthright do to me?" (Gen. 25: 32).

> "Lest there be any fornicator, or profane person, as Esau, who for one morsel of meat sold his birthright" (Heb. 12: 16).

3. Balaam was in bondage to Money.

> "Woe unto them! for they have gone in the way of Cain, and ran greedily after the error of Balaam for reward, and perished in the gainsaying of Core" (Jude 11).

4. Demas was in bondage to the World.

"For Demas hath forsaken me, having loved this present world, and is departed unto Thessalonica; Crescens to Galatia, Titus unto Dalmatia" (2 Tim. 4: 10).

5. Korah was in bondage to Position.

"And they gathered themselves together against Moses and against Aaron, and said unto them, Ye take too much upon you, seeing all the congregation are holy, every one of them, and the Lord is among them; wherefore then lift ye up yourselves above the congregation of the Lord?" (Num. 16: 3).

6. Nadab was in bondage to Intemperance.

"Do not drink wine nor strong drink, thou, nor thy sons with thee, when ye go into the tabernacle of the congregation, lest ye die: it shall be a statute for ever throughout your generations" (Lev. 10: 9).

7. The Samaritan was in bondage to Unbelief.

"Then a lord on whose hand the king leaned answered the man of God, and said, Behold, if the Lord would make windows in heaven, might this thing be? And he said, Behold, thou shalt see it with thine eyes, but shalt not eat thereof."

"And that lord answered the man of God, and said, Now, behold, if the Lord should make windows in heaven, might such a thing be? And he said, Behold, thou shalt see it with thine eyes, but shalt not eat thereof. And so it fell out unto him: for the people trode upon him in the gate, and he died" (2 Kings 7: 2, 19, 20).

THE AFFLICTION OF ISRAEL

1. Did not hinder progress.
2. Proved morally helpful.
3. United the nation.
4. Purged away the dross.
5. Prepared them to accept a deliverer.

THE BABE IN THE BULRUSHES

(Exod. 2: 1-10)

1. *A Death Decree.*—Pharaoh, king of Egypt, had decreed the death of every male child, born to Hebrew parents in Goshen. This edict was in force when the babe Moses was born to Amram and his wife, of the tribe of Levi— born under the death sentence. In like manner Satan, of whom Pharaoh is the type, has compassed the ruin of mankind, by sin, which brings death (Rom. 5: 12). Herod's edict for the death of the Bethlehem babes was another of Satan's plans (Matt. 2: 11), to destroy the infant Savior.

2. *A Mother's Faith.*—Fearless of the king's wrath (Heb. 11: 23), and strong in her confidence towards God, Moses' mother hid the baby three months, and God, as always, honoured her faith and preserved her "goodly child," who was fair to God (Acts 7: 20, marg.), and destined to be Israel's deliverer. "God moves in a mysterious way."

3. *The Ark of Bulrushes.*—Unable longer to hide the babe in the house, the mother prepared a cradle of bulrushes, lined it with "pitch"—the same word as in Exod. 30: 12, translated "ransom," emblematic of Christ's atonement (1 Tim. 2: 6), and putting into it her helpless babe, committed it to flags on the brink of the Nile. Here we have a picture of a sinner safe in Christ.

4. *"Drawn Out."* At the command of Pharaoh's daughter, God's chosen instrument for his preservation, the weeping babe is raised to new life, beyond death, out from it, to be under royal protection, cared for and preserved for God's service. So the believing soul is safe from wrath (Rom. 5: 9), drawn out from death (John 1: 24), "raised up" to new life (Eph. 2: 6), to serve God (Rom. 6: 11).

Illustration. — Rowland Hill remarks, "Little Moses was safer in his cradle of bulrushes on the banks of the Nile, with alligators all around, than if he had been in his mother's bosom. For the eye of God was over him, and the arm of God was shielding him, night and day."

THE CHOICE OF MOSES

Moses, learned in all Egypt's wisdom, mighty in words and deeds, goes forth to look on the ill-treatment of his people, and is moved with compassion for them. But they knew him not, nor received his intervention on their behalf (Acts 7: 24, 25). So the Lord Jesus came to His own, but His own received Him not (John 1: 11), nor did they own Him as their deliverer and ruler (Luke 19: 14).

1. *A Noble Choice.*—With every prospect of worldly advancement, the reputed son of Pharaoh's daughter, Moses deliberately and "by faith," having confidence in the Word of God, as to his people's redemption and deliverance, cast in his lot with the despised and downtrodden Israelites in Goshen, forsaking Egypt, and taking his place among the "people of God," esteeming the reproach for Christ, greater riches than Egypt's treasures, looking onward to the final recompense. Thus it is, that the Christ-won heart, in view of the riches of Christ, the blessedness of being His, and the sharing of the reproach for Him, with His people, gives up the world (Phil. 3:18).

2. *Saved to Serve.* — Moses was saved, "drawn out," and

called to serve his God. He stands the honored servant, "faithful" to God (Heb. 3: 5), doing His will, refusing to lower His standard or compromise His demands (Exod. 8: 26, 27; 10: 9-25) in any measure. And God blessed and owned his service. So ever does firm decision, faithful service, and full obedience, please God (1 Sam. 15: 22, 23).

3. *A Rich Reward.*—A great deliverance (Exod. 14: 31), a song of triumph (Exod. 15: 1), a place of nearness to God (Exod. 19: 20), an honored burial (Deut. 34: 6), and a place with Christ in glory (Mark 9: 4), were the recompense for all Moses gave up in that day.

Illustration.—Donald Ross used to say, "God gives salvation for nothing, and handsomely pays His saved ones for all that they do and suffer for Him here, for He will be no man's debtor."

A BUSH BURNING WITH FIRE

When Pharaoh sought for Moses to slay him, he fled into the land of Midian, where he became a keeper of sheep to Jethro the priest. From the place of a prince in the palace of Egypt, to that of a shepherd in the desert, was indeed a descent, a change of circumstances. But in these humble surroundings he was to learn of God, and become fitted to be the deliverer of His people. The Lord Jesus took a humble place in human life, so that He might reach and save sinners (Phil. 2: 7).

1. *The Burning Bush.*—This strange sight, which arrested the attention of Moses, and which he turned aside to see, was evidently the symbol of Israel as a nation. They were in the "furnace of Egypt" (Deut. 4: 20), and yet they were not consumed, for the more they were afflicted, the more they grew (chap. 1: 12). As a Gospel picture, the fire would speak of God's holiness (Heb. 12: 20). Moses

fearing and trembling—a sinner owning his unfitness to approach to God; the voice of God revealing Himself as a Deliverer and Savior.

2. *God's Promise.*—The promise given to Moses was one of unconditional grace, embracing deliverance from Egypt and entrance into Canaan. The Gospel of the grace and glory of God includes deliverance from wrath (1 Thess. 1: 10), the world (Gal. 1: 4), justification (Rom. 3: 24), entrance into the heavenlies (Eph. 1: 3; 2: 6), sanctification and glorification (Rom. 8: 30) with Christ.

3. *Moses Commissioned.* — Here, before the bush that burned, Moses is called and commissioned to be the messenger to and deliverer of Israel. To him God gives the promise of His presence with him, a word to cheer surely to all who know their own weakness and His strength (2 Cor. 12: 9, 10), for life and service.

Illustration.—When the persecutors of the Scottish Covenanters burned Patrick Hamilton, their first martyr, at the stake in St. Andrews, the effect on halting Christians was to bring them to decision. A wit, which was in the service of the prelate who was the chief instigator of the martyrdom, said to his master, "If any more are to be burned, burn them in the cellar, for the smoke of Patrick's fire, has infected all on whom it blew."

THE BURNING BUSH

I. A Bush.
  1. Overlooked.
  2. Despised.
  3. Insignificant.
  4. Small.
  5. Worthless in itself.
  6. Perishing.
  7. Weak.
  (1) Israel. (2) The Church. (3) Believers.

II. In the Desert.
 1. Dreariness.
 2. Barrenness.
 3. Exposed to tempests.
 4. Exposed to storms.
 5. Exposed to wild beasts.
 THIS DESERT THIRSTY WORLD
III. Burned with Fire.
 1. Purification.
 2. Cleansing.
 3. Refining.
IV. But NOT Consumed.

EXCUSES OF MOSES

1. Personal unworthiness.
 "Who am I?" (Exodus 3: 11).
2. Insufficiency and ignorance.
 "What shall I say?" (Exodus 3: 13).
3. The unbelief of the people.
 "They will not believe" (Exodus 4: 1).
4. Wilfulness of the people.
 "They will not hearken" (Exodus 4: 1).
5. Lack of Eloquence.
 "I am not eloquent" (Exodus 4: 10).
6. Unwillingness of mind.
 "Oh, my Lord . . . send . . . . "
 i. e., anyone (Exodus 4: 13).

THE PRESENCE AND POWER OF GOD

"Certainly I will be with thee" (Exodus 3: 12).
1. Then the work must succeed.
 Success is assured.
2. Then there need be no lack of power.
3. Then grace is sufficient.

THE DIVINE NAME "I AM"
Exodus 3: 13-15

1. Self-existence.
2. Causative energy.
3. Eternity.
4. Personality.
5. Fidelity.
6. Covenantal Grace.
7. Mystery.

THE ROD OF MOSES

(Type of Divine Power in the hands of Faith)

1. Made dead things live
    (dry sticks became serpents).
2. Made living things die
    (water into blood).
3. Punished the wicked
    (by plagues).
4. Made a way where there was no way
    (Red Sea).
5. Destroyed the ungodly
    (drowned).
6. Wrought miracles.
7. Defeated the enemies of God's people.

"WHAT IS THAT IN THINE HAND?"
(Exodus 4: 2)

1. Moses with his dry stick (Rod).
2. Shamgar and his ox goad.
3. David with his sling and stones.
4. Ehud and his dagger.
5. Samson with the jawbone of an ass.
6. Jael with the hammer and nail.
7. Widow and her two mites.

8. Dorcas with her needle.
9. Mary with the alabaster box.
10. Naaman's maid.
> "What is that in thine hand?"

THE GOSPEL ACCORDING TO MOSES
(Exodus 6: 6-8)

1. Redemption:
   > "I will redeem you."
2. Deliverance:
   > "I will rid you out of bondage."
3. Regeneration:
   > "I will bring you OUT."
4. Acceptance:
   > "I will take you to me."
5. Assurance:
   > "Ye shall KNOW."
6. Rest:
   > "I will bring you from under the burdens.
7. Sanctification:
   > "I will bring you IN."

THE GREAT HAIL STORM
(Exodus 9: 13-26)

The plagues sent by God on the land of Egypt may be used to illustrate the more terrible judgments yet reserved for this world (see Rev. 6: 9). In Pharaoh and his people, we have a type of the sinner who opposes his will to God's, and although often reproved becomes hardened.

1. GOD'S WARNING.—Before the storm of hail came down, God in mercy warned the Egyptians of its approach, and told them to find shelter for man and beast. In mercy, God warns sinners now (Job 26: 18; 2 Thess. 1: 7-9), telling them of a place of refuge provided in Christ, where all may find safety and security (Isa. 32: 2; Heb. 6: 18).

2. SHELTER SOUGHT.—"He that feared the word of the Lord" sought shelter for himself, his servants, and cattle (verse 20). So with men today. Those who believe God's testimony concerning judgment to come, flee to Christ, and find shelter. When Noah heard of judgment coming, he was "moved with fear and prepared an ark" (Heb. 2: 7). The truth of judgment to come is used by God to awaken the conscience and rouse the sinner to a sense of his danger. All who have come to Christ are "in Him" (Rom. 8: 1), and safe from judgment to come (1 Thess. 1: 10).

3. EXPOSED TO THE STORM.—When the storm descended, it found (notwithstanding God's warning) those who had failed to seek shelter for themselves and their cattle. "Sudden destruction" (1 Thess. 5: 3) overtook them. How solemn a thing it is to despise God's Word! As it was in Israel's day, so surely will it be in ours (Acts 13: 40). Despisers will perish, procrastinators will reap the bitter harvest of their folly. Let all who fear the Lord, and believe His Word, lift up the warning cry, and tell of "the Man" who is the one Hiding-Place of God's providing (Isa. 32: 2).

Illustration.—In a great May storm among the Scottish mountains, a widow carrying her only child was overtaken, and seeking the shelter of a rock, wrapped her child in a shawl, covering him with all the raiment she could spare, then facing the storm to seek a better shelter for herself and her loved one. Next day the mother was found in a snowdrift dead, the child alive, sheltered and warm, in the crevice of the rock.

> "Rock of Ages, cleft for me,
> Let me hide myself in thee."

DEATH OF THE FIRSTBORN

Notwithstanding all the judgments God had brought upon Egypt, still Pharaoh hardened his heart, and drove Moses from his presence, saying, "See my face no more, or thou shalt die." Evidently he treated God's long-suffering as slackness, as many do today, to their eternal loss.

1. *"One Plague More."* — Mercy despised brings heavier judgment. The last plague was the death of all the first-born of Egypt, their hope, the chief of their strength (Psa. 78: 51). All, of every rank, prince and slave (verse 5) fell under the stroke of God. Mercy had lingered long, but was despised; now comes judgment, swift and awful. All who harden their neck, against God (Prov. 29: 1), and reject His Son as Savior, will come under His judgment.

2. *In the Night.* — The awful judgment came when least expected. In the midnight hour, all Egypt was suddenly awakened out of sleep to find their first born dead. Sinners are asleep. Judgment will come in such an hour, as they think not (Matt. 26: 44), "as a thief in the night" (2 Pet. 3: 10).

3. *A Wail of Despair.* — When the Egyptians awoke and found themselves under judgment, there was a great cry; but it was too late, for judgment had already fallen. Egypt weeps, but it is of no avail. Pharaoh's last refuge of lies had been swept away, and he and his people exposed to judgment. In Matt. 25: 6 we are told of another "midnight cry" yet to be heard, when the door of mercy is found to be closed forever, and some are found outside.

4. *Pharaoh's Prayer.* — "Bless me also" (chap. 12: 32) was Pharaoh's prayer. Too late he had seen his folly, but there was no blessing for him now. He had despised God

and His messenger, and in him the righteous God was about to set forth a monument of His "power" (Rom. 9: 17) in retribution for wrongdoing and wrath for grace abused.

Illustration.—"One dance more and defiance to the fire," cried a young officer in a brilliantly lit ballroom in Moscow, when warned that the city was on fire. And that "one dance more" cost him and all the gay company, their lives. For the fire had reached the fortress and an explosion ended the dance.

THE LAMB CHOSEN AND SLAIN
(Exod. 12: 1-6)

At the commandment of the Lord, Abib—which was the seventh month of the ordinary year—became the first month of Israel's year. It was a new beginning, founded on redemption, the beginning of a new reckoning. So it is with the redeemed and regenerated sinner. All things "become new" (2 Cor. 5: 17; 1 Pet. 4: 2, 3).

1. *The Lamb Chosen.*—"Every man a lamb," a lamb for an house. Individual sinners need a Savior, and the whole household of God is founded on redemption. The Lord Jesus was the Lamb chosen by God (1 Pet. 1: 20), and manifested in due time as Sacrifice and Savior.

2. *The Lamb Described.*—"Without blemish." Such was to be the lamb chosen for the passover. Of the Lamb of God it is written, He was holy, harmless, undefiled (Heb. 7: 26). "He knew no sin." "He did not sin" (2 Cor. 5: 31). And in death He offered Himself "without spot" to God, as an acceptable sacrifice.

3. *The Lamb Slain.*—The Lamb thus chosen, must die—"without shedding of blood is no remission" (Heb. 9: 22). The perfect example of Christ in life could not meet the demands of God's throne, or the sinner in his need. It

was through His death that He "obtained redemption" (Heb. 9: 12). The redeemed in heaven sing, "Thou wast slain, and hast redeemed us to God by Thy blood."

4. *Between the Evenings* (v. 6, marg., with Deut. 16: 6). There was just time to sprinkle the blood, and secure the household, before the judgment fell. The Gospel of God's grace, the story of redeeming love, is God's last message to the world, before His judgment comes upon it.

Illustration.—"I am spotted as a leopard, but I have a spotless Savior," was the confession of a saved Indian.

THE FIRST-BORN UNDER THE BLOOD
(Exod. 12: 1-23)

It was to be a "night much observed" that "night of the Lord" (v. 42). And so indeed it was to all generations. For it was the night of the Israelites' redemption by blood, deliverance by power, severance from Egypt, and farewell to bondage—the whole from first to last a living parable of man's ruin and God's remedy, of sin and salvation as described in the Word and made known in the Gospel.

1. *A New Start.*—"The beginning of months" (v. 1). An old year suddenly broken off, a new year is begun. So by redemption and regeneration the believing sinner passes from the old into the new, out of death into life, out of darkness into light. The greatest day in a human life, one to be "much observed" is conversion's day.

2. *God's Death Sentence.*—"I will smite all the first-born." Terrible words! God spake them: He fulfilled them. "The Lord smote ALL the firstborn" (v. 29): prince and slave, none escaped. It was the wages of sin — death (Rom. 6: 23). In earlier judgments life had been spared, Israel in Goshen was exempt; but here, there is no mitigation, "no difference" (Rom. 3: 23).

3. *A Way of Escape.*—For Israel a redemption was provided, a way of escape marked out by God. It was His own ransom (Job 33: 24), a way of His choosing. Redemption by blood is that way: then in type, now in fact. "The Lamb of God" (John 1: 29) has come. His blood is precious blood.

4. *The Blood Shed and Sprinkled.*—A lamb, without blemish, is chosen, proved, sacrificed, slain. Its blood preserved, is sprinkled with a bunch of hyssop on the lintel above and the side posts of each Israelite dwelling. The family enter through, and under the sprinkled blood, and there abide immune from death, in life, feasting in peace, girded and ready to leave the land of bondage for the fair fields of Canaan, at God's bidding. The picture is complete: it is God's own type of redemption by the blood of Christ (1 Pet. 1: 19), which as believers we HAVE (Eph. 1: 7) now. The blood appropriated made the Israelite safe—as safe as God could make him. The uttered word, "I will pass over you" (v. 13) made him sure—as sure as God is true.

5. *All Safe.*—At midnight the judgment came. Not a house in Egypt without death. Under the blood, all were in life. Outside all was judgment; inside all was peace. So "in Christ," trusting in Him (2 Tim. 1: 12), in His blood (Rom. 3: 25), there is present salvation, no condemnation (Rom. 8: 1). Outside Christ (Eph. 2: 12) there is condemnation (John 3: 18), and upon all such, "sudden destruction" cometh (1 Thess. 5: 1,2).

A LAMB WITHOUT BLEMISH
(Exodus 12: 5)

In this familiar story, we have the great Redeemer in His perfections in life, atoning death, and the value and use of His blood set forth in type. The instructions regarding the choice and condition of the lamb, the period of its remaining with them, and, finally, the time and manner of its death, all point forward to Jesus, "the Lamb of God," by whom and in whose blood (Eph. 1: 7) redemption is procured. This is the grand theme of the great Gospel story.

1. *A New Beginning.* — The month Abib (Deut. 16: 1) (which Josephus tells us was the seventh month of the year), became, by the commandment of God, the first month to Redeemed Israel. The first six months of the year were thus, as it were, blotted out, and God made a new beginning with the nation, bringing them into a new relationship with Himself. From this point the new history of Israel begins. A sinner's new birth, through faith in Christ (Gal. 3: 26), is to him the dawn of a new era, the beginning of a new life (2 Cor. 5: 17), The past is blotted out and forgotten (Heb. 10: 17; 1 Pet. 4: 23), and all things become new.

2. *The Lamb Chosen.*—"Every man a lamb"—"a lamb for an house." As individuals, sinners need a Savior. Each must have one, being able to say, "my Savior" (Luke 1: 46). "Who loved ME and gave Himself for ME" (Gal. 2: 20). The church, the aggregate of the redeemed, is purchased by His blood (Acts 20: 28). "Jesus is the Lamb," foreordained before the foundation of the world (1 Peter 1: 20). He was manifested in God's due time (1 Tim. 2: 6; Rom. 5: 6). The time between the tenth and fourteenth days, may point to the earthly life of Christ, from Bethlehem to Calvary, during which time He was proclaimed the "Lamb of God."

3. *A Lamb without Blemish.* — Without spot, outwardly without blemish inwardly. Such was Jesus (1 Pet. 1: 19). He was "holy, harmless, undefiled" (Heb. 7: 27). His foes confessed that they could find no fault in Him (John

19: 4). A "male of the first year," insuring strength and fulness of vigor. The Lord Jesus was Perfect Man and the Mighty God in one Person. His person gives value to His work. To deny His Divinity, or to impeach His manhood, is to rob the Son of God of His glory and the Gospel of its power. To deny the Son is to be without the Father (1 John 2: 21), to have no God and no hope.

THE LAMB SLAIN
(Exodus 12: 6, 7)

The incarnation, death, and resurrection of the Lord Jesus, are the three great foundation truths upon which the Gospel rests. To disturb any one of them is to weaken the whole fabric. Not only was the passover lamb to be chosen, set apart, and proved perfect, but it must be slain. The life lived was not enough. The perfect example of the Lord Jesus could not reach the sinner. He must die. "He offered Himself without spot to God" (Heb. 9: 14), in order to obtain our redemption, and release us from the power of sin.

1. *The Death of the Lamb.*—It was to be killed "in the evening," between the evenings (margin). The Hebrew day had two evenings (see Lev. 23: 32). From sunset to sunset: it began with the first and ended with the second. Jesus dies at the completion of the ages (Heb. 9: 27). After the death of the lamb, there was sufficient time to sprinkle the blood, and secure the safety of the household, before the awful midnight judgment fell. "The Gospel of God concerning His son" (Rom. 1: 2), the tidings of Christ crucified, is God's last message to men. Then will come the judgment.

2. *Sprinkling the Blood.*—The blood of the lamb was shed. This was the ground of all that followed—safety, redemption, liberty. The death of Christ is the ground of every blessing the believing sinner receives. The blood was held

in a bason, and by a bunch of hyssop, it was sprinkled on the lintel and doorposts of Israel's houses, as Jehovah had instructed them. There His eye saw it as He passed through the land.

3. *Safe Beneath the Blood.*—Having sprinkled the blood, they were to pass under it, through the door into the house. The death of Christ has to be appropriated by faith individually for salvation. The hyssop, by which the blood was applied, is a figure of that repentance and faith which appropriates salvation.

A BLOOD—SPRINKLED DOOR
(Exodus 12: 22, 23)

1. *The Blood of the Lamb.*—The shedding of the blood was the ground of all that followed. Safety, redemption, deliverance, liberty, are all secured by the death of Christ. In His blood there is redemption, forgiveness (Acts 13: 39), present peace (Col. 1: 20), and future glory (Rev. 5: 9).

2. *Appropriation.*—It was not enough that the lamb should be slain, the blood must be used, applied to the door posts and lintel by "a bunch of hyssop." It is by the individual sinner appropriating the death of Christ, that he is saved: "through faith in His blood" (Rom. 3: 25).

3. *Sprinkling the Blood.*—Of Moses, the Holy Spirit has written, "By faith he kept the passover and the sprinkling of the blood" (Heb. 11: 28). Israel's sprinkling of the blood was an evidence of their faith, and the appropriation of the means of salvation God has provided (Rom. 10: 9), brings to us salvation.

4. *The Assuring Word.*—The sprinkled blood made the Israelites safe, the uttered Word of God made them sure. For the believer there is no condemnation (Rom. 8: 1). The blood is between him and judgment.

5. *Strength.*—Feeding on the roast lamb—type of communion with a suffering Christ—gave strength for their journey. None were "feeble" (Psa. 105: 37) among them.

6. *The Midnight Judgment.*—Judgment came when least expected. At midnight all Egypt was awakened by the awful stroke of God. Thus, suddenly, when men sleep, shall their judgment come (1 Thess. 5: 3).

7. *A Great Cry arose over all Egypt.* A louder wail awaits guilty Christendom.

Illustration.—A simple countryman who had trusted in Christ, testified, "I am under the blood, and as safe as God can make me. Can anything beat that?"

THE SHELTERING BLOOD
(Exodus 12: 1-33)

Exodus 12 is an early edition of the Gospel of Christ.

1. *Condemnation*—"I will smite all the firstborn."
   The sentence of death was passed upon all the first born. All were condemned already. There was no difference between the Jew or Egyptian. All the first born were under sentence of death. In each and every house there must be a dead person or a dead lamb.

2. *Substitution*—"Every man a lamb."
   Either a firstborn or an innocent lamb must die. No escape. "Behold the lamb of God." "If ye believe not ye shall die."

3. *Appropriation*—"Ye shall TAKE the blood."
   The blood of the lamb must be *applied*. Israel was not saved by the death of the lamb, but by the blood of the lamb. There must be a personal acceptance and a personal appropriation.

4. *Salvation*—"When I see the blood I will *pass over* you."
   NOT when I see the people (Israelites),

NOT when I see the Egyptians,
NOT when I see the Lamb;
BUT when I see the BLOOD.
The blood made them *safe* while the promise made them *sure*.

5. *Separation* — "Ye shall put away *leaven* out of your houses."
   Leaven is typical of that which is *evil*. All secret sin must be put away. It must be put away immediately, i. e., "Even the first day." Repentance and regeneration settle the sin question for ever.

6. *Obedience*—"None of you shall go out until the morning." Under the sheltering blood they must remain. As Noah must remain within the Ark and as Rahab must remain inside the house, so Israel "shall not go out until."

Continued safety lies in continued obedience. There is no such thing as once in the ark always in the ark; or once in the house always in the house; or once in grace always in grace. Noah, Rahab, Israel must abide as well as enter for continued safety depends on continued obedience.

7. *Victory*—"Rise . . . go . . . take . . . be gone."
   Leave all and possess all. Give all and receive all. As *condemned* sinners we must *appropriate* Christ as our *substitute*. Keep *separated* and *obedient,* and *salvation* and *victory* will be ours.

DELIVERANCE

I. The cruel taskmasters.

    1. Their motive (fear).

    2. Their conduct (cruel).

    3. Their great sin (ingratitude).

       (Joseph saved the Egyptians from death.)

II. The crying people.
    1. Their sufferings.
    2. Their helplessness.
    3. Their groans.
III. The Gracious God.
    1. Heard their cry.
    2. Raised up Moses.
    3. Delivered them.

FAITH ILLUSTRATED IN MOSES
(Hebrews 11)

"By faith Moses, when he was born, was hid three months of his parents, because they saw he was a proper child; and they were not afraid of the king's commandment. By faith Moses, when he was come to years, refused to be called the son of Pharaoh's daughter; choosing rather to suffer affliction with the people of God, than to enjoy the pleasures of sin for a season; esteeming the reproach of Christ greater riches than the treasures in Egypt; for he had respect unto the recompense of the reward. By faith he forsook Egypt, not fearing the wrath of the king: for he endured, as seeing him who is invisible. Through faith he kept the passover, and the sprinkling of blood, lest he that destroyed the first-born should touch them. By faith they passed through the Red sea as by dry land which the Egyptians assaying to do were drowned" (Heb. 11: 23-29).

verse
1. The Refusal of faith, "Refused" 24
2. The Choice of faith, "Choosing" 25
3. Calculation of faith, "Esteeming" 26
4. Prospect of faith, "Recompense" 26
5. The Separation of faith, "Forsook Egypt" 27
6. Courage of faith, "not fearing" 27
7. The Feast of faith, "kept the passover" 28

EIGHT TYPES OF FAITH

1. Justifying faith ....ABEL
2. Translating faith ....ENOCH
3. Separating faith ....NOAH
4. Sacrificing faith ....ABRAHAM
5. Self denying faith ....ISAAC
6. Sanctifying faith ....JACOB
7. Overcoming faith ....JOSEPH
8. Enduring faith ....MOSES

THE SHELTERING BLOOD
(Exodus 12: 1-32)

1. Condemnation:
   (all condemned).

2. Substitution:
   "Ye shall take every man *a lamb*."

3. Appropriation:
   "Ye shall TAKE the blood."

4. Salvation:
   "When I see the blood."

5. Purification:
   "Put away leaven."

6. Resignation:
   " . . . until the morning."

7. Separation:
   "Take your flocks; be gone."

"In an American town under fire during the civil war, the general commanding the Federal army proclaimed that all the inhabitants who came under the shelter of the Federal flag would be safe, protected by the same power as would destroy the enemy. So it is with those 'under the blood'."

THE PASSOVER . . . CHRIST

(Exodus 12)

The distinct and direct blessings which came to Israel were a foreshadowing of similar blessings in Christ which come to all believers.

1. Remission of Sins.

   "For this is my blood of the New Testament, which is shed for many for the remission of sins" (Matt. 26: 28).

2. Redemption.

   "In whom we have redemption through his blood, the forgiveness of sins, according to the riches of his grace" (Eph. 1: 7).

3. Reconciliation.

   "And having made peace through the blood of his cross, by him to reconcile all things unto himself; by him, I say, whether they be things in earth, or things in heaven" (Col. 1: 20).

4. Purification.

   "How much more shall the blood of Christ, who through the eternal Spirit offered himself without spot to God, purge your conscience from dead works to serve the living God!" (Heb. 9: 14).

5. Access.

   "For when Moses had spoken every precept to all the people according to the law, he took the blood of calves and of goats, with water, and scarlet, wool, and hyssop, and sprinkled both the book, and all the people" (Heb. 9: 19.

6. Made nigh.

   "But now in Christ Jesus ye who sometimes were far off are made nigh by the blood of Christ" (Eph. 2: 13).

7. Communion.

"The cup of blessing which we bless, is it not the communion of the blood of Christ? The bread which we break, is it not the communion of the body of Christ?" (1 Cor. 10: 16).

8. Victory over Egyptians.

"And they overcame him by the blood of the Lamb, and by the word of their testimony; and they loved not their lives unto the death" (Rev. 12: 11).

THE PASSOVER
(Exodus 12)
A Complete Type of Divine Redemption.

1. Sentence of death pronounced against all in the land of Egypt.

"And Moses said, Thus saith the Lord, About midnight will I go out into the midst of Egypt: And all the first-born in the land of Egypt shall die, from the first-born of Pharaoh that sitteth upon his throne, even unto the first-born of the maid-servant that is behind the mill; and all the first-born of beasts" (Exodus 11: 4, 5).

The first-born typifies the natural man.

"Howbeit that was not first which is spiritual, but that which is natural; and afterward that which is spiritual" (1 Cor. 15: 46).

The first-born typifies all men in Adam.

"Wherefore, as by one man sin entered into the world, and death by sin; and so death passed upon all men, for that all have sinned" (Rom. 5: 12).

2. There was only one way of escape.

"Speak ye unto all the congregation of Israel, saying, In the tenth day of this month they shall take to them every man a lamb, according to the house of

their fathers, a lamb for an house" (Exodus 12: 3).
"The next day John seeth Jesus coming unto him
and saith, Behold the Lamb of God which taketh
away the sin of the world!" (John 1: 29).

3. The lamb was sufficient for all.

"They shall take of them every man a lamb" (Exodus 12: 3).

Salvation is individual NOT social.

4. The blood of the lamb must be applied.

"And they shall take of the blood, and strike it on
the two side posts and on the upper door post of
the houses, wherein they shall eat it" (Exodus 12:7).

1. A Lamb.
2. A slain Lamb.
3. The Blood of the slain Lamb.

"Purge out therefore the old leaven, that ye may be
a new lump, as ye are unleavened. For even Christ
our passover is sacrificed for us" (1 Cor. 5: 7).

5. After the blood was applied they were to feast on the
slain lamb.

"And they shall eat the flesh in that night, roast with
fire, and unleavened bread; and with bitter herbs
they shall eat it" (Exodus 12: 8).

"Then Jesus said unto them, Verily, verily, I say
unto you, Except ye eat the flesh of the Son of man,
and drink his blood, ye have no life in you. Whoso
eateth my flesh, and drinketh my blood, hath eternal
life; and I will raise him up at the last day. For my
flesh is meat indeed, and my blood is drink indeed.
He that eateth my flesh, and drinketh my blood,
dwelleth in me, and I in him. As the living Father
hath sent me, and I live by the Father; so he that

eateth me, even he shall live by me" (John 6:53-57).

(1) They were to feast with girded loins:
"And thus shall ye eat it; with your loins girded, your shoes on your feet, and your staff in your hand; and ye shall eat it in haste: it is the Lord's passover" (Exodus 12: 11).
The girdle is a symbol of service.

(2) With staff in hand and shoes on the feet. Ready to walk and climb.

(3) Eat in haste.
Canaan was their goal NOT Shur, Marah, Elim, Horeb, or Kadesh.

CROSSING THE RED SEA
(Exodus 14: 1-23)

Satan never yields his captives without a struggle. Here, in Pharaoh and his host pursuing the escaping people, we have a picture of the power of Satan seeking to retain and to recapture, if possible, those whom God would set free. But God is now for His people, and against their foes.

1. *Pharaoh in Pursuit.*—All the chariots of Egypt join in the chase. He who underrates the power of Satan, and speaks lightly of his devices, is ignorant of his power. The power of God alone is able to defeat the mysterious might of Satan, and that power is FOR and IN all who believe (Rom. 8: 32) and are born of God (Eph. 3: 20).

2. *Israel's Extremity.*—The wilderness had shut them in. It was vain to look around for help. God only could deliver. So the sinner must learn and own his helplessness, abandon all creature resources, and "look" (Isa. 14: 22) to God alone for salvation. In their extremity "they cried unto the Lord." It was the cry of conscious need, the appeal of souls "without strength" (Rom. 5: 6).

This is the moment when God makes Himself known. He sends the word that stills all fear (v. 13).

3. *The Divided Sea.*—"The Lord caused the sea to go back." The mind of man could never have conceived such a way of escape. Jehovah alone could cleave a pathway through the waters, so that what seemed certain death, became to them a path of life. Such was the Cross of Christ. Apparent defeat; yet there, in the scene of Satan's apparent triumph, He was vanquished, and his power brought to nought (Heb. 2: 14).

4. *Deliverance from Pharaoh.*—Thus God delivered Israel from Pharaoh's power. Sinners need deliverance from sin's dominion, as well as its punishment. They need emancipation from the authority of Satan (Acts 26: 18), as surely as safety from wrath to come (1 Thess. 1: 10). Both are found in Christ. The blood of Christ secures the one, the power of God the other.

Illustration.—In the harbor of Troon, there lie three great German submarines being dismantled and destroyed. Only a year or two ago, they were the terror of the seas; now their power is broken and their glory departed. A witness surely, that defeat and disaster have overtaken the proud empire they served.

All who fight against God and against God's will shall be broken.

THE PILLAR OF FIRE

Pillars are emblems of the strength, support, power, and presence of God.

1. The Pillar of Blessing.

"And Jacob rose up early in the morning, and took the stone that he had put for his pillows, and set it up for a pillar, and poured oil upon the top of it" (Gen. 28: 18).

2. The Pillar of Strength.

"And he set up the pillars in the porch of the temple: and he set up the right pillar, and called the name thereof Jachin; and he set up the left pillar, and called the name thereof Boaz" (1 Kings 7: 21).

3. The Pillar of Truth.

"And when James, Cephas, and John, who seemed to be pillars, perceived the grace that was given unto me, they gave to me and Barnabas the right hands of fellowship; that we should go unto the heathen, and they unto the circumcision" (Gal. 2: 9).

4. The Pillar of Warning.

"But his wife looked back from behind him, and she became a pillar of salt" (Genesis 19: 26).

5. The Pillar of Guidance.

"And it came to pass, as Moses entered into the tabernacle, the cloudy pillar descended, and stood at the door of the tabernacle, and the Lord talked with Moses" (Exodus 33: 9).

THE JUSTICE AND RIGHTEOUSNESS OF GOD EXHIBITED IN THE DESTRUCTION OF PHARAOH

Pharaoh—

1. was cruel,
2. was a murderer,
3. was a despot,
4. refused his subjects leisure for worship,
5. sinned against God,
6. sinned against humanity,
7. hardened his heart,
8. was a hard taskmaster,
9. openly defied God,
10. was insolent, egotistic, conceited,

11. was a liar
(Pharaoh refused to keep his promises),
12. was doomed
(Pharaoh was a type of the devil).

THE SPECIFIC SINS OF MEN

1. Pharaoh ....Hardened his heart.
2. Cain ....Envy
3. Ham ....Lewdness
4. Nimrod ....Fame
5. Lot ....Wealth
6. Sarah ....Pride
7. Esau ....Pleasure
8. Isaac ....Venison

"GO FORWARD"
(Exodus 14: 15)

1. Go forward to Canaan (holiness).
2. Go forward through obstacles.
3. Go forward in triumph.
4. Go forward because God commands it.
5. Go forward, for the Holy Spirit leads.
6. Go forward, for all the Old Testament saints encourage us.
7. Go forward, for to stand still means stagnation.
   "Stand still" only to find the will of God, then
   "Go forward" in implicit obedience.

THE SONG OF MOSES
(Exodus 15: 1-2)

The first recorded song in the Bible is a song of salvation. Bible religion is a singing religion. Singing has thus a chief place in the service of the saved. As another has said, "Salvation and song, like Siamese twins go together. With the work of Luther, Wesley, and Moody came streams of new songs of praise."

The song of Moses was:

1. A song of Redemption.

   God had delivered them from Egypt and from Pharaoh, and they celebrate their deliverance by singing and dancing.

2. A Song of Praise.

   "Moses sang this song unto the Lord." Here was a spontaneous pouring forth of jubilant praise to God, who had overwhelmed His and their foes and emancipated them for ever.

3. A song of Testimony.

   "*I* will sing . . . the Lord is *my* strength and song. . . . he is become *my* salvation: he is *my* God . . . and *I* will exalt him" (v. 2).

   David could say, "The Lord is *my* shepherd." Bible salvation is a personal, experiential salvation which voices itself in testimony, for "*with the heart* man believeth and *with the mouth* confession is made unto salvation."

SALVATION AND SONG
(Exodus 15: 1, 2)

Salvation and song are Siamese twins.

1. A Song of Redemption.
2. A Song of Victory.
3. A Song of Praise.
4. A Song of Testimony.
5. A Song of Consecration.
6. A Song of Holiness.
7. A United Song.

MIRIAM, THE SINGER
(Exodus 15: 20, 21)

1. *Salvation Wrought.*—The Lord saved Israel (chap. 14: 30). Their deliverance was "the salvation of the Lord" (chap. 14: 13). He did the work: they "stood still" and saw it. Their enemies were overcome: they sank as lead in the waters. "Then believed they His Word, they sang His praise" (Psa. 106: 12). "Salvation is of the Lord" still: it is "His salvation" by gift (Titus 2: 10), "our salvation" by believing (Eph. 1: 13).

2. *Salvation's Song.*—The first song in the Bible, sung by a nation of saved ones, is found in Exodus 15. The singers were those who had seen "the salvation of the Lord," and knew they were "saved from the hand of the enemy." So now, it is the one who has known forgiveness of all his iniquities (Psa. 103: 1-4) who calls on his soul to "bless the Lord." It is he whose feet have been taken from the pit and set upon a Rock, who has the new song in his mouth (Psa. 11: 3).

3. *Miriam's Praise.*—Miriam, the sister of Moses and Aaron (Ex. 11: 4; Num. 26: 56), led the women of Israel's praises—probably a song additional to that of the whole company—and their song was of Jehovah's power. No other subject is worth our praise. The world's songs are vapid, time worn, tame, as compared with the triumphs of the Lord in redemption and salvation.

4. *Miriam's Silence.*—In Numbers 12 we read of this same Miriam, who sang the Lord's song, using her tongue in speaking against her brother Moses. And for this sin God smote her with leprosy. She had then to be severed from her people, and shut out in silence until she was healed. The same tongue may give forth "bitter and

sweet" (Jas. 3: 9-10). Let us watch our words, and use our tongues only for the praise of God and the spread of His truth.

A SONG OF SALVATION
(Exodus 15: 1-23)

1. *Saved to Sing.*—God's redeemed are a singing people (Psa. 107: 2). This is the first song recorded in Scripture. It was sung by a redeemed people on the shore of the Red Sea. It is the song of a people set free from captivity, delivered from their enemies, and conscious of God's salvation.

2. *When to Sing.*——They "saw, they believed, they sang" (Psa. 106: 12). Before redemption, sinners "sigh and cry" (Ex. 2: 23) for deliverance. When they "see the salvation of the Lord" (chap. 14: 13-31), they sing (comp. Isa. 12: 1, 2). So sings the believer, who knows his feet have been taken from the mire and the clay and set upon a rock (Psa. 11: 1-3). When Samaritan sinners were saved, there was "great joy" in that city (Acts 8: 8). When the Ethiopian was saved, he went on his way rejoicing (Acts 8: 37).

3. *The Subject of the Song.*—"The Lord is my strength and song. He is become my salvation." It is all about the Lord. What He is, what He has done. Nothing of self at all. This is the song of a sinner saved by grace, on earth and in heaven. Self has no credit, no glory. Salvation is all of grace, all of God.

4. *Present Grace and Future Glory.*—The song looks back to a past deliverance, praises God for present grace, and looks onward to future glory. It begins in grace and ends in glory (see Psa. 84: 5-11). When earth's songs have

all been sung, and its memories gone, the heavens will ring with salvation's new song through eternal ages.

5. *Redeemed, Led Forth, Guided* (v. 13).—The Redeemed are a separated (Gal. 1: 4), led (Psa. 23: 2, 3), and guided people (Psa. 32: 8).

Illustration.—Billy Bray the Cornish Miner said, "I sing as a lark in the sunshine of heaven."

THE START ON THE WAY
(Read Exodus 15: 22-27)

After triumph there is frequently trial. Delivered from the power of the enemy, the children of Israel pass into the wilderness with its trials. The life of the Christian is made up of light and shade, joy and sorrow, but the end is peace. We consider today the first trial of the children of Israel and its effect upon them.

1. *Israel's First Trial.* "They went out into the wilderness of Shur, and found no water" (v. 22). The want of water was their first difficulty. Everything up to this point had been in their favor. All the money in the world cannot purchase a shower of rain. They were entirely dependent upon God, and this was a splendid opportunity for seeking a supply from a good God. This reminds us that all our blessings (temporal and spiritual) come from God, and reach us because of Christ's atoning sacrifice.

2. *Their Bitter Disappointment.* "When they came to Marah, they could not drink of the waters" (v. 23). After three days' travel in a hot, dry desert, it must have been a real joy to find water. But, alas, what disappointment! It was so bitter they could not drink it. The one who drinks at earth's cisterns is doomed to disappointment. Christ alone gives the water of life that thoroughly

satisfies (John 4: 14). His invitation is, "If any man thirst, let him come unto me and drink" (John 7: 37).

3. *Their Ungrateful Murmuring.* "The people murmured against Moses" (v. 24). Trial tests the reality of our profession, and discovers both to God and ourselves what kind of people we are. Instead of turning to God as they should, they murmur against Moses. And so a chapter which opens with triumphant song, ends with discontented murmuring (v. 24). Oh! the unbelief of the human heart.

4. *God's Healing Tree.* "The Lord showed him a tree" (v. 25). The casting of the tree into the waters made them sweet. This would remind us of the Lord Jesus being cast into the deep waters where the floods overflowed Him (Psa. 60: 2) in order that all the blessings of salvation might be ours. Calvary's tree changes the bitter sense of judgment into the sweetness of forgiveness.

5. *God's Gracious Provision.* "They came to Elim, where were twelve wells of water" (v. 27). The wilderness has its Elims as well as its Marah's. The children of Israel found delight and satisfaction at the cool refreshing springs of Elim. The believer today finds his joy and satisfaction at the "wells of salvation" (Isa. 12: 3). Indeed he has within him a well of water "springing up" (John 4: 14), also seventy palm trees, i. e., shelter . . . protection . . . shade . . . comfort. Go on and you too will have YOUR Elims.

Illustration.—Sir Andrew Clark, the favorite physician of Queen Victoria, once said: "There is but one remedy for all the spiritual diseases in this world of ours, and that remedy is the person and work of the Lord Jesus Christ."

THE HEALING TREE
(Exodus 15: 22-25)

1. A tree.
   "He bare our sins in His own body on the tree."
2. Made known or revealed by God.
3. Needful.
4. Near at hand.
5. Accepted.
6. Turned bitterness into sweetness.
7. A tree to be remembered.
   (This do in remembrance of me.)

FOOD FOR THE JOURNEY
(Exodus 16: 1-15)

Our subject is the feeding of the children of Israel in the wilderness with manna from on high.

1. *A Murmuring People.* "The whole congregation . . . murmured" (v. 2). A little more than a month on the way, their provisions became exhausted, and instead of asking God for supplies they murmured against God's servants. Murmurers have bad memories. The Israelites forgot their deliverance from Egyptian bondage, the passage of the Red sea, the sweetening of Marah's waters, and Elim's refreshing springs. They forgot past mercies, and when trial crossed their path they refused to trust God for future provision. The root cause of their murmuring was unbelief.

2. *A Gracious God.* "I will rain bread from heaven for you" (v. 4). God did not bring His people into the wilderness to starve them. He not only leads His people; He also feeds them. Like all other blessings, the manna came down from heaven. The Lord Jesus is the true Bread

from Heaven (John 6:32), of which if a man eat he shall live for ever.

3. *A Necessary Condition.* "The people shall go out and gather a certain rate every day" (v. 4). It was God's part to send the manna; it was the people's part to gather. In Egypt, the lamb had not only to be slain, but the blood had to be applied. The application of the blood to the door-posts and lintel made them safe from judgment. The gift of God is eternal life, but if we are to be saved the hand of faith must be put forth to accept that gift.

4. *A Passing Opportunity.* The manna had to be gathered daily, and in the morning, because when the sun waxed hot it melted (v. 21). Just as the body must be fed regularly to keep it in health, so the child of God must feed his soul daily on the bread of life. Yesterday's supply will not do for today. Then, again the manna was to be gathered early in the morning. The believer should begin the day with God. Our blessed Lord could say: "He wakeneth mine ear morning by morning to hear as the learned" (Isa. 50:4). For the unconverted, the lesson is that they should seek Him now for tomorrow may be too late (see Prov. 8:17 and 2 Cor. 6:2).

5. *An All-Sufficient God.* "At even the quails came up" (v. 13). The quail was a bird about the size of a turtle dove. God brought the quails to the camp of Israel, showing that He could not only create a new thing in the manna, but that He is also above nature. He can use and control all nature to supply His people's need.

Illustration.—Frederick Douglas, the great slave orator, was speaking at a time when things looked very dark for his people. In a melancholy tone he exclaimed: *"The white man is against us, Governments are against us, I see no hope for the*

colored race. I am full of sadness." Immediately a poor
old colored woman in the audience rose, and said, *"Frederick,
is God dead?"* The question electrified the people, and they
broke forth in songs of praise, glorifying God. The Children
of Israel forgot that the living God was among them (Joshua
3: 10).

MANNA AND ITS MEANING

(Exodus 16: 1-17)

When Israel entered the wilderness, God fed them with
"bread from heaven." Its name was "manna." Rained down
every morning for forty years, it ceased only when they
reached the land of corn and wine.

1. *Israel in Need of Bread.*—The bread they carried with
   them out of Egypt soon was gone, and there was none in
   the wilderness. Hungry and faint (Psa. 118: 5), the
   people cried to God, and He who hears the ravens call,
   said, "I will rain bread from heaven." A sinner needs a
   Savior. God has provided and sent One (John 3: 17)
   down to where he is (1 Tim. 1: 15).

2. *Daily Bread for the Redeemed.* — Christ is also the
   "Bread of God" for His own (John 6: 33). Every morning it came down, lying white and pure upon the dew
   (Num. 10: 9). To the taste it was sweet. In all this, it
   is a lovely type of Christ, the Lowly One, spotless in
   purity (Heb. 7: 26), abiding in sweetness (Psa. 119: 10).
   As the lamb in Egypt represents Christ in death, and the
   old corn of the land (Josh. 7) Christ risen, so the manna
   points to Christ as the lowly One, the Servant of Jehovah,
   and perfect Examplar of His own (Phil. 2: 4-8).

3. *Gathered and Eaten.*—God "sent" the manna, but the
   people had to gather it. So with Christ. God gave His
   Son (John 3: 16). Sinners must "receive" Him, in order to be saved (John 1: 12). The Word tells of Him

welcomed and believed (Acts 2: 41). And the Word of God must be read (1 Tim. 4: 13), fed on (1 Pet. 2: 2), and enjoyed (Jer. 15: 16), meditated on (Psa. 1: 3) for daily food, by the child of God.

4. *The Manna Despised.*—Grumbling against it, began with "the mixed multitude," camp-followers, not of Israel. Quickly the infection spread, until Israel united with them in their demand for Egypt's food. The manna was first "despised" (v. 6) and later "loathed." So Christ is by some neglected, by others rejected, and the Word of God set aside for earthly pleasures and worldly desires.

MANNA

I. Names:

    1. God's Manna
    2. Bread of heaven
    3. Bread from heaven
    4. Corn of heaven
    5. Angels' food
    6. Spiritual meat
    7. Manna

The expression Bread of Heaven sets forth Christ as the food of all the hosts of heaven. All heaven feasts on Christ. He is the Bread of God, for God feasts on Him. He is the Bread of Angels, for angels feast on Him. He is the bread of life, for believers feast on Him. Apart from Him there is hunger and thirst. He alone can satisfy.

II. Description:

    1. Like Coriander Seed.

        The idea meant to be conveyed by the word *coriander* is that manna (Christ) will expel all the gas, bluster, bombast, and self importance from the soul of the believer. A good dose of coriander seed, *manna*, will settle the talkativeness, gossip, slander, and backbiting of the Christian Church.

2. Seed.
   This speaks of life. The mustard seed of the parable may be small but it is HOT and LIVING. Christ is the living bread sent down from heaven.

3. White.
   This typifies the spotless purity of Jesus Christ.

4. Sweet.
   Here is set forth the nourishing, ineffable sweetness of Jesus Christ.

5. Came down in the night.
   That speaks of the *Humiliation* of our Lord Jesus Christ, who came down in the night of this world's history. Gross darkness filled the world when Jesus was born.

6. Fell upon the dew.
   Dew, like water, fire, salt, wind, and oil is a type of the Spirit. Christ was conceived and born of the Holy Spirit.

7. Gathered every morning.
   The first business of the day. We are to seek first the Kingdom of God.

8. It was given in answer to prayer.
   Ask and ye shall receive.

9. It was given for forty years.
   The number forty (40) is the number of testing. There is sufficient in Christ for the whole period of our earthly life of testing and conflict. It teaches us that man cannot live by bread alone.

10. It was ground and made into cakes.
    The grinding and beating and pounding and kneading typify the sufferings of Christ in order to provide bread for the famishing soul of man.

11. It was baked in pans.
    The fire necessary to the cooking of these cakes typifies the anger of God against sin which burned against Jesus Christ as the sin bearer.

12. It was despised by many.
    Christ has always been despised by the many. The Church is yet a little flock. Few there be that find Him.

13. Those who despised were punished.
    Christ is a Savour of death unto death to those who loathe and despise the heavenly manna.

14. Neglect meant death.
    To neglect gathering the manna because of carelessness, laziness, indifference, or pre-occupation resulted in certain death.

What marvelous pictures of the heavenly manna! What matchless foreshadowings of the grace and goodness of God in providing heavenly food for earthly ingrates such as we.

MANNA

The Antitype as Seen in the Type (John 6: 31-35)

1. I will rain bread from heaven.
   I am the Living Bread which came down from heaven.

2. When the dew fell . . . the manna fell upon it. (Dew a type of the Holy Ghost as communicator and embodiment of the blessing.)
   The Holy Ghost shall come upon thee, and the power of the Highest shall overshadow thee, therefore also

that holy thing which shall be born of thee shall be called the Son of God.

3. There lay a small, round thing, as small as hoar frost, and white.

> Small—Humility. Laid in a manger; no room in the inn. A carpenter's son.
>
> Round—Consistency, evenness. All the elements of lovely character in perfect balance.
>
> White—Purity, without spot.

4. It tasted like wafers made with honey.

> Sweet—Good tidings of great joy. They wondered at His gracious words.

5. Like fresh oil.

> Peace on earth.
>
> Full of grace.

6. It lay on the ground.

> Lowliness—He made Himself of no reputation.

7. It fell round about the host.

> Within reach of all.

8. It was ground, beaten in a mortar, and baked.

> "He was wounded for our transgressions. . . . "
>
> "By His stripes we are healed."

9. All had sufficient—an omer for every man.

> "He that cometh to me shall never hunger."
>
> (None came short.)

10. This is the bread the Lord hath given you to eat.

> "My Father giveth you the true bread from heaven."

MANNA
Type of Christ (John 6: 49, 50).

1. Came down.
2. Came down from heaven.
3. Came down in the night (time of darkness).
4. Came down on the dew (type of the Holy Spirit).

5. Was white (holiness).
6. Was round (no sharp corners or rough edges).
7. Was sweet.
8. Was like seed (life).
9. Must be appropriated.
10. Neglect meant weakness and death.
11. It was the bread of angels.

      Christ is the bread of:

          1. God;
          2. Angels;
          3. Israel;
          4. Life to all.

12. It was God provided and God sent.
13. It was given to the undeserving and was free.
14. It was despised.
15. Was to be gathered early.
16. Suitable for young and old.

MANNA
OR
WHAT IS IT?

1. Small ....Despised, Isa. 53: 3
2. Round ....No points, Phil. 2: 7
3. Sweet ....Christ perfect, Heb. 2: 5
4. Lay on the ground ....Humble, Matt. 11: 29
5. Adapted for all ....For the whole world, 1 John 2: 2
6. Came upon the dew .....The Holy Spirit, 1 Peter 1: 12
7. Fell by miracle ....By miracle of grace, Rom. 5: 20
8. The bread of the mighty

        Feeding on Christ makes strong, John 6: 57

9. When not used, bred worms and stank

        Day by day, 2 Cor. 4: 16

10. No MANNA where Christ not preached ....Gal. 1: 8, 9

WATER FROM THE ROCK
(Exod. 17: 1-7)

Israel in a desert, parched and dry, thirsting for water which they could not find, is a striking picture of sinners in the present world. There is nothing to slake their soul thirst, nothing to satisfy the heart. "Shall thirst again" (John 4: 13) is written upon all earth's pleasures. In hell, thirst will remain, with nothing to quench it.

1. *The Rock in the Desert.*—"That Rock was Christ" (1 Cor. 10: 4)—type of Him who, while on earth, was "despised and rejected" of men, yet the Lifegiver (John 5: 22-24). In Horeb, a flinty rock (Psa. 114: 8) was the chosen source, from whence the stream of life would flow. To it Moses led the people; in it alone was their hope.

2. *Smitten by the Rod.*—Smitten by the rod of Moses, the rock gave out its stream. Jesus, "smitten, stricken, and afflicted," becomes the fountain of life to sinners (John 3: 14). Apart from His death there could be no life, no salvation, for the lost. From Him the water of life flows (John 7: 37).

3. *The Water of Life.*—That flowing stream meant life to Israel. Jesus had life in Himself (John 5: 26), and through His death, that life becomes "the free gift of God" to all (Rom. 6: 23), for "whosoever will" (Rev. 22: 17).

4. *Drink and Live.*—The thirsty Israelite had only to stoop down, and drink and live. So sinners are invited to "come," to "take" it freely. Drinking he lives; he has life—it is "in him," a well too (John 2: 14) springing up to its Source in heaven.

5. *Speak to the Rock.*—In days which followed, as they journeyed through the wilderness, the word was, "SPEAK ye to the rock" (Num. 20: 8). Christ in glory, never

again to be smitten in death, is the Source of all blessing. His people have but to "speak" to, to ask from Him, and of His fulness they receive.

Illustration.—When Fred Stanley Arnot first crossed the great Khalahari desert, he suffered much from thirst. No water could be found anywhere. All in a moment, the Zambesi river came into view, and after drinking of it without stint, he sat down and sang, gazing on its flood flowing on unused, while men perished of thirst.

WATER ON THE JOURNEY
(Exodus 17: 1-15)

Our lesson is full of beautiful gospel truth. We have to consider the smitten rock and the plenteous supply of water which followed Israel all through the way.

1. *Israel's Ungratefulness.* "The people did chide (strive or contend) with Moses" (verse 2). Arriving at Rephidim, there was no water, and immediately the people begin to chide Moses. In chiding Moses they were blaming God. They actually blame Moses for bringing them into the wilderness to kill them. God had just begun to rain bread from heaven, and when their need of water arose, instead of appealing to Him for a supply, they speak of God as a heartless monster. The Israelites were no worse than many today, who seem to think of God in the same way. God is the great Giver. He has given *the best of heaven* for *the worst of earth* (John 3: 16).

2. *God's Goodness.* "What shall I do with this people, they be almost ready to stone me?" (v. 4). Moses had done a great deal for the people, but like Paul in a later day, he could have said, "The more abundantly I love, the less I be loved" (2 Cor. 12: 15). They treated our Lord in the same shameful manner. On one occasion they would

have stoned Him (John 8: 59). They did worse, "they crucified Him" (John 10: 18). Notwithstanding their treatment of Moses, God in the richness of His grace supplies their need.

3. *God's Righteousness.* "Thou shalt smite the rock, and there shall come water out of it" (v. 6). The people deserved to have been smitten by the rod of judgment because of their heartless unbelief; but instead the word was "smite the rock." Paul tells us, "that Rock was Christ" (1 Cor. 10: 4). The incident is a beautiful type of Jesus Christ, the Rock of Ages, smitten at Calvary, in order that the blessing of salvation might flow to men. Happy is he who can sing truthfully: "Rock of Ages, cleft for me."

4. *Salvation's Fulness.* "He smote the rock, the waters gushed out" (Psa. 78: 20). Like salvation the supply was plenteous and continuous. It followed them all the way. We are reminded that the blessing of salvation is for "whosoever will," and can be had "without money and without price" (Isa. 55: 2). Christ was smitten; the Holy Spirit has come.

5. *Christ's Intercession.* "Then came Amalek and fought with Israel" (v. 8). Hitherto Israel had their battles fought for them. This was their first encounter with the enemy. Amalek is a type of the flesh, and immediately conversion takes place the flesh in the believer wars against the Spirit. Moses, Aaron, and Hur, on the Mount, remind us of our blessed Lord who continually maketh intercession for us (Heb. 7: 25). His hands never hang down with weakness or weariness. Prayer changes things.

Illustration.—The smiting of the rock clearly speaks of the substitutionary work of Christ on Calvary. "I thank Jesus that He was punished instead of me." Such was a little girl's confession of faith in Christ. It was simple, yet expressive; brief, but full of truth and meaning. It contained the sum and substance of salvation through a crucified Christ (Gal. 2: 20).

THE SMITTEN ROCK
(Exodus 17: 5, 6)

1. The Rock.
    1. Majestic.
    2. Strong.
    3. Speaks of stability and solidity.
    4. Stands the storms and tempests.
    5. Opposite to the yielding earth and shifting sands.
    6. Noted for its durability.
    7. Gives shelter and support to weary pilgrims.
II. The Smitten Rock.
    1. By God's Command.
    2. By the Rod of Moses (Law).
    3. Publicly.
    4. Once.
    5. Gave forth its water.
    6. Satisfied the need of all.
    7. Free.
    8. To neglect or reject meant death.

THE FIGHT WITH AMALEK
(Exodus 17: 8-16)

This was Israel's first battle, the first warfare of a redeemed people. God was about to teach them His way of warfare. Up to this point in their history, God had fought FOR them, now He was to fight THROUGH them.

1. *The Foe.*—The enemy was a distant kinsman of Israel (Gen. 26: 17), who had become a mighty people, dwelling in the wilderness. Amalek means "a people that lick

up," and this they sought to do when they attacked Israel. This conflict is typical of the conflict which every believer wages every day of his life. Pharaoh—a type of the world from which they had been delivered (Gal. 1: 3), but Amalek is still to meet. He is a type of the flesh, still in the redeemed as well as against them, and ever lusting "against the Spirit." This conflict begins after redemption (Eph. 1: 7), and salvation, and after the Spirit takes up His abode in the believer.

2. *His Tactics.*—The attack upon Israel was sudden and unexpected, evidently delivered from behind, for it reached the hindermost — the stragglers — first (Deut. 25: 17, 18). This reminds us that the deceitfulness of sin is most to be feared (Heb. 3: 1-13). Those who follow hard and press on are less likely to fall a prey to its devices. Those who faint and lag behind, are usually the first to fall under the deceitful power of sin.

3. *Moses the Intercessor.*—Moses, the leader of the people, went up to the mount, there to prevail with God for His people. A beautiful picture this of the Lord Jesus, who is now at the right hand of God interceding for His own (Rom. 8: 34).

4. *The Victory.*—Joshua—who represents the believer acting in the power of the Spirit in the use of the Word— handles the sword and so repulses the enemy. The sword of the Spirit (Eph. 6: 17) is the only weapon that will prove effectual in this conflict against self and sin, within, without, around, in all its forms.

Illustration.—A lad who had been converted, came to his teacher in great distress, saying, "I am very unhappy, for I fear I am not saved. There is such a fight going on in me, as if there were two of us, each pulling different ways." The teacher said, "Thank God. If there were no life, there would be no fight."

VICTORY is possible. DELIVERANCE may be ours THROUGH the Word and Prayer. Matt. 3: 11; 1 Thess. 5: 23, 24.

A FAMILY GATHERING
(Exodus 18: 1-12)

During the time of his mission in Egypt, Moses' wife and her two sons, had been in the house of her father—Jethro, the priest of Midian. When the news of Israel's redemption came to Jethro, he at once set out with his daughter and her sons to meet Moses, and to restore his family to him. It would be a happy meeting.

1. *The Story of Deliverance.*—Moses tells to Jethro (and we may surely infer his family also) the deliverance God had wrought for Israel, and how Pharaoh had been destroyed. Thus is the Christian to testify of Christ's redemption, God's salvation, and his own conversion (Psa. 78: 4-13) first among his own "friends."

2. The Bride. — Zipporah, the daughter of Jethro, was Moses' wife, given to him during the days of his rejection, when he fled to Midian. In this aspect, she appears as a type of the Bride given to Christ during the time of His rejection by the world, to be presented to him in the day of His return.

3. *Gershom and Eliezer.*—Such were the names given to the sons of Moses. Gershom means "a stranger there," typical of the believer while on earth. Eliezer, "whom God helps," true of the believer now, as it will yet be of Israel. He will be their Deliverer (Zech. 14).

4. *Jethro Worships.*—Upon hearing from Moses the story of what God had wrought for Israel, Jethro rejoices and wor-

ships God, dispensationally, pointing on to the time of millennial blessing, when Jews and Gentiles will worship God together, and walk in His ways (Isa. 2: 2, 3). And in this time it shows how grace works in families—"thou and thy house" (Acts 26: 32).

Illustration.—A family, sundered and scattered owing to the European war, lately met in the old home, and standing around the table, joined hands, singing, "Praise God from Whom All Blessings Flow." It was a touching sight.

The family of God will soon be united.

THE BURNING MOUNT
(Exodus 19: 1-16)

"The holiness of God" might be fittingly given as a heading to this chapter. God would teach His people Israel how far distant morally He was separated from them. Further, in this chapter they are for the first time put under law.

1. *A Holy God.* "Israel camped before the mount" (v. 2). Sinai's mount speaks of God's holiness. It was here that God manifested Himself and His holy character. Paul tells us that "He dwelleth in the light which no man can approach unto" (1 Tim. 6: 16). If holiness had been God's only attribute there would have been no salvation for man. But He is the God of all grace, and has manifested his abounding grace in the gift of His well beloved Son.

2. *A Fitting Mediator.* "Moses went up unto God" (v. 3). The bounds set round about Sinai, its thunders and lightnings all speak of the great moral distance existing between an holy God and a guilty sinner. Moses stood between the people and God, and he is a fitting type of the Lord Jesus Christ, the Mediator of the new covenant

(Acts 8: 6), through which we approach God today (Heb. 10: 19).

3. *A Great Deliverance.* "I bare you on eagle's wings" (v. 4). The eagle is emblematic of strength. When her young are in danger the eagle will carry them on its pinions to a place of safety. The Lord by a strong hand delivered His people from Egyptian bondage, and destroyed their enemies. He brought them unto Himself. We are reminded that Christ not only died to save us from sin's guilt, but also to bring us to God (1 Peter 3: 18). Like the Israelites, we may be in the wilderness, but like them we have God, and "if God be for us, who can be against us?"

4. *A Conditional Covenant.* "If ye will obey my voice indeed, and keep my covenant, then ye shall be," etc. (v. 5). The old covenant had an "if"—a condition. The new covenant of grace has no conditions for the sinner, because all the conditions have been fulfilled for him by the Lord Jesus Christ. All that a sinner has to do to be saved eternally is to trust Christ. "It is of faith that it might be by grace" (Rom. 4: 16).

5. *A Thankful People.* "Ye shall be unto me a kingdom of priests and an holy nation" (v. 6). "We are a holy priesthood to offer up spiritual sacrifice" (1 Peter 2: 5), the sacrifice of praise to God, giving thanks to His name (Heb. 13: 15).

Illustration.—The difference between law and grace is tersely put in the verse from an old book:

"Run, John, and live, the law commands,
  But gives me neither legs nor hands
  Yet better news the Gospel brings,
  It bids me fly, and gives me wings."

THE TEN COMMANDMENTS
(Exodus 20: 1-20)

Parallel Scriptures: Acts 7: 35; Rom. 3: 19, 20.

Israel had entered the wilderness and arrived at Sinai. Here they received from God, through Moses, His law, which they accepted and pledged themselves to keep. "The law is holy, just, and good," showing the exceeding sinfulness of sin, but it gives no power to enable us to keep it. Thus the commandment which was ordained to life, is found to be unto death.

1. *The Law Given.*—Moses went up into the mount, while the people stood at a distance from God. Christ is the one Mediator (1 Tim. 2: 5). By His Cross reconciliation is effected (Rom. 5: 9), and the Gospel proclaims a way of access by His blood (Heb. 10: 19).

2. *The Law Broken.*—Notwithstanding Israel's promise to "do" all that the Lord had spoken, they soon broke that promise, and brought the curse of a broken law upon them (Deut. 28: 14-20). Man by nature is a sinner, and a broken law makes him a transgressor (Rom. 4: 5). The law brought fear and trembling to those who received it. The Gospel brings peace and joy to all who believe it.

3. *The Law Magnified.*—The law failed to bring blessing, because man could not keep it. The Lord Jesus "magnified it" (Isa. 42: 21) in His life, and died to remove its curse (Gal. 3: 10). He has satisfied its demands, and now remission in His name (Acts 10: 43) and redemption through His blood (Eph. 1: 6) are made known.

4. What the Law Cannot Do.—It could not justify (Rom. 3: 20); it cannot save (Titus 3: 3). By works, none are

justified (Rom. 3: 20), none are saved (Eph. 2: 9). Nor by law and grace, faith and work combined. Salvation is by grace alone (Eph. 2: 8), without effort and apart from merit.

Illustration.—"Your religion is all DOING, and never DONE. Mine began by resting on a finished work, the work of Christ. You work FOR salvation to earn it. I work FROM salvation, because I have it," was the recent testimony of a young believer.

LOVE IN THE TEN COMMANDMENTS
(Exodus 20)

1. Supreme love to God makes "other gods" impossible.
2. Love never consents to represent the object of its affection by a bird or a beast or a serpent.
3. Love never takes "The Name" in vain.
4. Love delights to reverence the "Lord's Day."
5. Love sanctifies and happifies the home.
6. Love can never consent to hurt, injure, or kill.
7. Love destroys lust.
8. Love prevents lying lips. Love will stop the voice, or pen of slander.
9. Love gives and sacrifices, but never steals.
10. Love has no covetous eyes for his neighbors' possessions, but seeks the welfare of all.

THE LAW REVEALED IN EXODUS

1. *The Moral Law.*

   This law reveals God as a Holy God and sin as exceeding sinful.

2. *The Ceremonial Law.*

   This law reveals God as a Saving God; saving from sin and its consequences.

3. *The Civil Law.*

      This law reveals God as a Just God, making it possible for a nation to live together and develop a Divine, universal religion.

The Moral Law deals largely with God.

The Ceremonial Law deals with sin.

The Civil Law deals with righteous living.

OUTLINE STUDIES OF THE TABERNACLE

1. The place where God MEETS the sinner.
   "THERE I will meet with thee" (Ex. 25: 22).
2. The place where God COMMUNES with the sinner.
   "There I will commune with thee" (Ex. 25: 22).
3. The place where God REVEALS himself to men.
   "And I will dwell among them and be their God" (Ex. 29: 45).
4. The place where God makes himself KNOWN (assurance).
   "And they shall know that I am the Lord" (Ex. 29: 46).
5. The place where God SPEAKS to men.
   "I will speak there unto thee" (Ex. 29: 42).
6. The place where God accepts the sinner.
   "It (the lamb) shall be accepted for .him (the sinner) (Lev. 1: 4).
7. The place where God FORGIVES the sinner.
   "It shall be forgiven them" (Lev. 4: 20).
8. The place where God RECEIVES FROM the sinner.
   "None shall appear before me empty" (Ex. 23: 15).

All this is true in connection with Christ, who tabernacled here among men.

In Christ and in Christ alone and through Christ only can God

> meet with
> commune with
> reveal himself to
> speak to
> accept
> forgive
> receive from

the sinner.

THE ALTAR OF BURNT OFFERING

1. Made of Wood.

    Wood is obtained from a living tree which has been cut down. This typifies Christ as the living, upright tree of righteousness, who was cut down, hammered, and nailed in order that He might provide a meeting place between God and man.

2. Overlaid with brass or copper.

    Brass is that which will endure the hottest fire and it typifies the righteousness, justice, and holiness of Christ enduring the fiery anger of God's wrath against sin.

3. Foursquare and with grating half way.

    The grating was thus on a level with the Mercy Seat and also the table of shewbread, which speaks to us of the Mercy of God being equal to the extent of sin and judgment.

    FOURSQUARE takes in the whole world — North, South, East, and West—for God so loved the world that he gave a tabernacle to Israel typifying that mercy was as high as sin and judgment. Grace is really greater than all our sin.

4. An inclined ascent but no steps.

    No steps were allowed, for God abominates the exposing of the body of a person. Inclined ascent for we are always ascending when we go God's way.

5. Large enough to contain all the vessels of the Holy Place. All the vessels of the Tabernacle could be accommodated within the limits of the Altar of burnt offering; thus typifying that IN CHRIST there is room for all and that within the one great sacrifice on the cross every other is comprehended.

6. It was Holy unto Jehovah and the distance from the East to the West was the distance between judgment at the altar (East) and Mercy in the Most Holy (West).

   "As far as the East (entrance of the tabernacle) is from the West (the Mercy Seat) so far . . . "

7. The ashes denoted acceptance. Christ's sacrifice was accepted and we are accepted in HIM.

God's twofold provision for cleansing was (1) at the altar of brass (blood); (2) at the Laver (water), thus typifying the cleansing of the heart from sin as an act of God's grace in our sanctification, and the constant cleansing by the water of the Word as we walk in the light.

THE VAIL

The Vail separated the Holy Place from the Most Holy Place.

1. It typified the humiliation and incarnation of Christ.

   "The vail . . . His flesh" (Heb. 10: 20).

   The unrent vail was seen at Bethlehem, at Nazareth, at the Jordan, and during the ministry of Christ.

2. Prophecy of its future rending.

   "He must go unto Jerusalem and suffer and be killed" (Matt. 16: 21).

3. The rent vail typified the death of CHRIST by crucifixion.

   The vail sets forth His birth. The rent vail sets forth His death. "From the top to the bottom" typifies the hand of God, for it pleased Jehovah to bruise Him.

4. The vail was rent to make man's access to God a possibility.

Christ died to bring us to God.

5. The vail was hung on four pillars.

Matthew, Mark, Luke, and John were thus typified as the pillars upholding Him who tabernacled among men. The four evangelists hold up to view the God of the Old Testament, who was manifested in the flesh.

The *year* of Christ's death was foretold by Daniel:

"After three score and two weeks shall Messiah be cut off" (Dan. 9: 25, 26).

The *day* of Christ's death was foretold in the Passover, i. e., April 14th (see Ex. 12).

The *hour* of Christ's death was typified in the daily offering of the incense and the evening sacrifice, i. e., three p. m. Thus it was foretold not only that He would die but that he would die on Thursday afternoon at three o'clock on April 14th. It was at the ninth hour that Christ died and while His body was being rent by the soldier's spear, the vail of the temple was being rent by the hand of God and thus was the door of Mercy and Grace flung open wide. The Priest was busy officiating before the temple vail when suddenly it was ripped from top to bottom. Thus is explained why many of the priests believed. Before the astonished gaze of the Priest the miracle was wrought, and, presto, he was convinced and went out and convinced others. Selah.

THE ARK

1. Made of Wood.

As wood is obtained from a living tree which has been cut down, so Christ was the living tree of righteousness cut down to provide a meeting place between God and man.

"That through death he might destroy him that had the power of death, that is, the devil" (Heb. 2:9-17).

2. Overlaid with Gold.

Gold comes from God and sets forth the Deity of Christ.

"I counsel thee to buy of me gold" (Rev. 3: 18), refers to us paying the price and obtaining something worth while which will stand the test of the judgment fires.

3. Went before the People of God.

"He goeth before them" (John 10: 4).

4. Its proper place was in the midst of God's people.

"There am I in the midst" (Matt. 18: 20).

"And in the midst one like unto the Son of man" (Rev. 1: 13).

5. Went down first into Jordan.

The word Jordan means death. Christ went down to death in order to make our death to sin a possibility.

"We are buried with him" (Rom. 6: 3, 4).

"Ye are dead" (Col. 3: 1-4).

6. God's people were to follow the Ark.

The command was given: "When ye see the Ark . . . go after it" (Josh. 3: 3).

The New Testament emphasizes this truth by urging us to look off unto Jesus (Heb. 12: 1, 2).

7. It brought down the walls of Jericho.

Before Christ all opposition shall crumble and the strongholds of sin and Satan shall be brought down.

8. When captured and taken by the foe, Israel forsook the Ark.

"They all forsook him and fled" (Mark 14: 50).

9. Brought death to the Philistines.

"Christ is a savour of death unto death" (2 Cor. 2: 15, 16).

10. Brought blessing to Obed-Edom.

Christ is a "Savior of life unto life" (John 14: 13).

11. Was carried by chosen men.

Saul of Tarsus, together with all the apostles, were chosen vessels "to bear my name" (Acts 9: 15).

12. Crossed the Cedron.

Christ went "over the brook Cedron" (John 18: 1).

13. Entered into proper place of rest in the Temple.

Christ is even now at the right hand of the majesty in the heavens.

14. Seen by John in heaven (Rev. 11: 19).

THE ALTAR AND THE BLESSING
(Exodus 20: 21-26)

It is remarkable that at the close of the great chapter (Exodus 20), in which the Law is given, God's commandment concerning the altar of sacrifice is found. The altar speaks, not of Law, but Grace. If man cannot come to God on the ground of his own righteousness, God will make a way of approach for him in His grace.

1. *The Altar of Sacrifice.*—God's appointed way of approach to Him is through the shedding of blood. This is still the royal road. There can be no other (Heb. 9). The new and living way (Heb. 10: 20) is the only way to God and heaven. All other ways lead to death and judgment.

2. *The Material Used.*—The altar was to be of earth or unhewn stone. A simple confession of the sinners' state and need. Neither man's art nor his efforts, can have any place in coming to God. There must be no steps to it. All are on a dead level, with no distinction (Rom. 3: 22, R. V.). All must come in the same way.

3. *The Place of the Altar.*—"In all places where I record my name, I will come to thee and I will bless thee." Blessing comes through sacrifice. It is bestowed in grace. How unlike the terrors of the fiery mount! At the Cross, God's love was manifested (1 John 4: 9, 10), and His righteousness proclaimed (John 3: 14-16). There too, He welcomes the sinner in righteousness.

4. *The Meeting Place.*—God meets the sinner as he is, without preparation or promised reformation. The Cross has given to God all that sin had taken from Him, and all that justice demands. The atoning death of Christ the Lamb of God is the cause of man's redemption and the channel through which God's grace reaches and saves all who believe in Christ.

THE DAY OF DECISION
(Exodus 32: 1-28)

One great decision, one eternal choice, is made by the soul when it accepts, trusts, and confesses Christ as Redeemer, Savior, and Lord. The link of union with Christ is formed (John 1: 41), a place "IN Christ" is found (Rom. 16: 7), and this abides for ever (John 10: 28).

1. *Testings.*—But for all truly born again ones, there are frequent testings, in which their faith is put on trial, and God proves them whether they will stand true to Him, and to His Word, should others fail. It was so in the day when the Lord spake the testing word to His professed disciples in John 6: 59, and when His foes surrounded Him to take Him (Matt. 26: 56). To stand true to God, His Christ, and His truth, when others fail or flee, is a signal honor, which the Lord does not forget (Rev. 2: 13).

2. *The Golden Calf.* Set up in the camp of Israel. Was a day of testing. It was no question then who were Israelites, but "Who is on the Lord's side?" The God of Is-

rael had been dishonored, an idol had been worshiped in the camp, where He also was. Moses had to make his decision as to his relation to God, and that which had been brought into His place. And standing at the gate he called aloud, "Who is on the Lord's side, let him come unto me." There was no middle course. For God with Moses, or in the camp with the idol, and against Him. And "all the sons of Levi gathered themselves together unto him" (v. 26). This was decision, this was God approved decision. So He ever does (Jer. 15: 19). He honors obedience, and sets apart the godly (Psa. 4: 8).

THE TWO BROKEN TABLES
(Exodus 32: 15-28)

We have to consider the sin of the children of Israel in setting up a golden calf and worshiping it. The weakness of Aaron's character is also manifested in submitting to the request of the people, whilst in Moses we see faithfulness to God displayed.

1. *Israel's Grievous Sin.* "Make us gods which shall go before us" (vs. 1 and 23). Moses had been in the mount with God for forty days, and the people became tired waiting his return. They could not believe in One they could not see. They first make a god, and then put their trust in it. They substitute a calf for Jehovah. Many such substitutes exist today. Men trust to gold, good deeds, anything and everything but Christ.

2. *Aaron's Great Weakness.* The people said unto Aaron, "Up, make us gods" (verses 1 and 23). Instead of taking a stand for God, Aaron, probably afraid of the people, not only gave way to their desire, but actually directed the movement. The fear of man bringeth a snare. Fear of their fellows keep many from Christ.

3. *Moses' Righteous Indignation.* "Moses' anger waxed hot, and he cast the tables out of his hands and brake them" (v. 19). Although Moses was a meek man, yet the idolatry of the people called forth his righteous indignation. It is possible to be angry and sin not (Eph. 4: 26). Moses' anger was aroused not on account of any indignity done to him, but because of the dishonor done to the Lord. The dashing to pieces of the new made tables of stone would speak of the effect of sin, destroying and marring God's handiwork.

4. *Sin's Bitter Consequences.* After burning the calf and strewing it upon the water, Moses made the people to drink of it (verse 20). "Whatsoever a man soweth that shall he also reap" (Gal. 6: 7). Sin must be punished either in the person of him who commits it, or in the person of God's appointed Substitute. Happy is he who can truly say from his heart: "He was wounded for my transgressions," etc. (Isa. 53: 5).

5. *Moses' Clarion Call.* "Who is on the Lord's side?" (verse 26). There were only two sides then; there are but two sides today—saved or unsaved. "He that believeth is not condemned: he that believeth not is condemned already" (John 3: 18).

Illustration.—There is a piece of ground at Gibraltar, situated between the British and Spanish possessions, which belongs to neither country, and it is called "neutral ground." There are many people today standing on what might be called "neutral ground." They say they are not saved, and they will not acknowledge they are lost. Men are either saved or lost. Moses' call was: "Who is on the Lord's side?"

TABERNACLE IN THE WILDERNESS
(Exodus 40: 1-16)

NOTWITHSTANDING their waywardness, God loved His people Israel, and His desire was to dwell amongst them. This was the reason why the tabernacle was set up in the wilderness.

1. *The First Anniversary.* "On the first day of the first month" (verses 1, 2). Exactly twelve months had elapsed since the celebration of the first passover in Egypt (Ex. 13: 2). God did not set up the tabernacle in Egypt. It was only after they were delivered by the blood of the lamb and freed from Egyptian bondage that God began to dwell amongst them. There can be neither acceptable worship nor service until the soul is sheltered under the blood.

2. *The Tabernacle of Testimony.* "Thou shalt set up the tabernacle" (verse 2). God is a God of fellowship, and "His delights are with the sons of men" (Prov. 8: 31). He must, however, have a dwelling place, the patterns of which are clearly defined by God Himself. If God is to be worshiped, it must be according to God's pattern. Much today that passes for worship never reaches God at all.

3. *The People's Gifts.* The tabernacle was built from material supplied by the people (Ex. 35: 20-29). They gave to God of their substance (Ex. 35: 20-29). First of all, God gives to us (John 3: 16), and then we give back to Him of His goodness (Psa. 23: 5).

4. *The Vessels in the Tabernacle.* There was (1) The Ark, called the Ark of Testimony; in it the tables of the law, on it the sprinkled blood, and above it the shekinah glory between the cherubim; (2) The Table, having on it the bread, twelve loaves, representing the twelve tribes;

this bread was eaten by the priests after it was accepted before God; (3) The Candlestick, made of gold, giving light from its seven lamps; (4) The Altar of Incense, overlaid with gold, from which the fragrant cloud arose before God; (5) The Altar of Burnt Offering, on which the sacrifice all for God was laid and consumed; (6) The Laver, at which the priests washed hands and feet before they entered on their work. All these again speak of Christ and His people. (7) The Mercy Seat.

5. *The Anointing Oil.* "Thou shalt take the anointing oil, and anoint the tabernacle, and all that is therein" (Ex. 40: 9). The vessels of the sanctuary represented different aspects of the work of the Lord Jesus Christ, and the anointing oil is typical of the Holy Spirit. We are reminded of the work of the Holy Spirit. Conversion is effected by the Spirit and the Word; and it is the indwelling Spirit that fits the believer for service (1 Cor. 6: 20). Pentecost supplies the Power.

Illustration.—Many people have no clearer notion of what true worship is than the dear old deacon who said: "Let us commence the worship of Almighty God by singing,

" 'Come, ye sinners, poor and needy,
Weak and wounded, sick and sore.' "

Singing such hymns is not worship. Worship is the outflow of a redeemed heart made divinely glad in the favor of God.

THE TABERNACLE
(Exodus 40: 17-35)

I. Its meaning:
"The shadow of heavenly things."
"The pattern of things in the heavens."
"The figures of the true."
Picture of "good things to come."

II. Its purpose:

"That God might dwell among them."

"God with us."

III. Its contents:

1. The Holy of Holies:
   1. The Ark.
   2. The Mercy Seat.
   3. The Incense Altar.
2. The Holy Place:
   1. The Candlestick.
   2. The Shewbread.
3. The Court:
   1. The Laver.
   2. The Brazen Altar.

THE BOARDS FOR THE TABERNACLE
(Typical of believers)

1. Rested on a foundation of silver.
   Silver speaks of redemption.

2. Natural life was given up.
   The boards were cut down. Like Saul on the way to Damascus, we must be cut down, severed from our old ways and works.

3. Each board was the same size.
   "Till we all come . . . unto the measure of the stature of the fulness of Christ."

4. Prepared.
   The boards were not only cut down but were planed, hammered, and polished to fit their own particular place in the tabernacle. Believers are prepared, throughly furnished.

5. Fitly framed together and clothed.

> The boards were covered with GOLD which typifies the believer clothed with the Holy Spirit (God).
> The individual boards joined together became one tabernacle as we are "All one in Christ Jesus."
> The Boards, standing upright in sockets of silver, typify the righteousness of believers in Christ and all having fellowship one with another.

———◆———

> *"Holy Bible, Book Divine,*
> *Precious treasure, thou art mine.*
> *Mine to tell me whence I came;*
> *Mine to teach me what I am;*
> *Mine to chide me when I rove;*
> *Mine to show a Savior's love;*
> *Mine art thou to guide my feet;*
> *Mine to judge, condemn, acquit;*
> *Mine to comfort in distress;*
> *Mine to lead to promises;*
> *Mine to warn of sinner's doom;*
> *Mine to say at cross there's room;*
> *Mine to show the living faith;*
> *Mine to triumph over death;*
> *Mine to tell of joys to come;*
> *Mine to bring an earnest home;*
> *Mine to point me out the road,*
> *Mine to lead my soul to God—*
> *Oh, thou precious Book Divine,*
> *Precious Treasure, thou art mine!"*

THE SUFFICING BIBLE

When I am tired, the Bible is my bed;
  Or in the dark the Bible is my light;
When I am hungry, it is vital bread;
  Or fearful, it is armour for the fight.
When I am sick, 'tis healing medicine;
Or lonely, thronging friends I find therein.

If I would work, the Bible is my tool;
  Or play, it is a harp of happy sound.
If I am ignorant, it is my school;
  If I am sinking, it is solid ground,
If I am cold, the Bible is my fire;
And it is wings, if boldly I aspire.

Should I be lost, the Bible is my guide;
  Or naked, it is raiment rich and warm.
Am I imprisoned, it is ranges wide;
  Or tempest-tossed, a shelter from the storm.
Would I adventure, 'tis a gallant sea;
Or would I rest, it is a flowery lea.

Does gloom oppress? The Bible is the sun.
  Or ugliness? It is a garden fair.
Am I athirst? How cool its currents run!
  Or stifled? What a vivifying air!
Since thus thou givest of thyself to me,
How should I give myself, great Book, to thee?

AMOS R. WELLS.